T0140889

EuroSPI² 2008

Software Process Improvement

Proceedings of the
EuroSPI 2008 Doctoral Symposium
Dublin, Ireland, September 2008

Editors
Rory V O'Connor
Fergal McCaffery

lero THE IRISH SOFTWARE ENGINEERING RESEARCH CENTRE

DCU

Editors

Rory V O'Connor
School of Computing
Dublin City University
Glasnevin
Dublin 9
Ireland
roconnor@computing.dcu.ie

Fergal McCaffery
Department of Computing
Dundalk Institute of Technology
Dundalk
Co. Louth
Ireland
Fergal.McCaffery@dkit.ie

Bibliographic information published by the Deutsche Nationalbibliothek

The Deutsche Nationalbibliothek lists this publication in the
Deutsche Nationalbibliografie; detailed bibliographic data are available
in the Internet at http://dnb.d-nb.de .

© Logos Verlag Berlin GmbH 2008
All rights reserved.

ISBN 978-3-8325-1952-0

Logos Verlag Berlin GmbH
Comeniushof, Gubener Str. 47,
10243 Berlin
Tel.: +49 030 42 85 10 90
Fax: +49 030 42 85 10 92
INTERNET: http://www.logos-verlag.de

Table of Contents

Acknowledgements

The Doctoral Symposium organisers acknowledge the generous financial support and assistance of the Office of the Vice-President for Research at Dublin City University and Lero, the Irish Software Engineering Research Centre (www.lero.ie).

In addition we acknowledge the support of the partners and members of the EuroSPI Initiative (www.eurospi.net) and of ISCN (www.iscn.com) in supporting this doctoral symposium.

SOFTWARE PROCESS IMPROVEMENT
EUROSPI 2008 DOCTORAL SYMPOSIUM

Rory O'Connor, School of Computing, Dublin City University, Dublin 9, Ireland, roconnor@computing.dcu.ie

Fergal McCaffery, Department of Computing, Dundalk Institute of Technology, Ireland, Fergal.McCaffery@dkit.ie

Abstract

This book constitutes the proceeding of the Doctoral Symposium of the 15th European Software Process Improvement Conference, EuroSPI 2008, held in Dublin City University, Dublin , Ireland in September 2008. The purpose of the EuroSPI Doctoral Symposium was to provide an opportunity for graduate students to present and explore their research interests under the guidance of a panel of distinguished experts in the field and to bring together Ph.D. students within the Systems & Software Process Improvement and Innovation field to discuss their research in an international forum.

1 EUROSPI OVERVIEW

EuroSPI is a partnership of research companies, experience networks and quality associations, with ISCN (International Software Consulting Network) as the co-coordinating partner. EuroSPI collaborates with a large number of SPINs (Software Process Improvement Network) in Europe.

EuroSPI's mission is to develop an experience and knowledge exchange platform for Europe where SPI practices can be discussed and exchanged and knowledge can be gathered and shared. This mission is implemented by three major action lines:

- An annual EuroSPI conference supported by Software Process Improvement Networks from different EU countries.
- Establishing an Internet based knowledge library, newsletters, a set of proceedings (research and experience tracks) and recommended books.
- Establishing an effective team of national representatives (in the future from each EU country) growing step by step into more countries of Europe.

The greatest value of EuroSPI lies in its function as a European knowledge and experience exchange mechanism for Software Process Improvement and Innovation of successful software product and service development. EuroSPI aims at forming an exciting forum where researchers, industrial managers and professionals meet to exchange experiences and ideas and fertilize the grounds for new developments and improvements.

1.1 The EuroSPI Conference Series

EuroSPI is a successful initiative since 1994. Annual conferences were held 1994 in Dublin (Ireland), 1995 in Vienna (Austria), 1996 in Brighton (UK), 1997 in Budapest (Hungary), 1998 in Gothenburg (Sweden), 1999 in Pori (Finland), 2000 in Copenhagen (Denmark), 2001 in Limerick (Ireland), 2002 in Nuremberg (Germany), 2003 in Graz (Austria), and 2004 in Trondheim (Norway), 2005 in Budapest (Hungary), 2006 in Joensuu (Finland), 2007 Potsdam (Germany), and 2008 in Dublin (Ireland).

EuroSPI conferences present and discuss results from software process improvement (SPI) projects in industry and research, focusing on the benefits gained and the criteria for success. Leading European universities, research centres, and industry contribute to and participate in this event. This year's event is the 15th of a series of conferences to which international researchers contribute their lessons learned and share their knowledge as they work towards the next higher level of software management professionalism.

1.2 The EuroSPI Doctoral Symposium

The 2008 conference represents the first time EuroSPI conference series has organised a Doctoral Symposium. The EuroSPI Doctoral Symposium mission is to provide an opportunity for graduate students to present and explore their research interests under the guidance of a panel of distinguished experts in the field. It is intended to bring together Ph.D. students within the Systems & Software Process Improvement and Innovation field to discuss their research in an international forum. The EuroSPI Doctoral Symposium will provide students with an opportunity to:

- Present their research work in a relaxed and supportive environment
- Receive constructive feedback and suggestions from peers and experienced researchers
- Gain an overview of the breadth and depth of research in the field
- Obtain insight into directions for research taken by other doctoral candidates
- Discuss concerns about research, supervision, the job market, and other issues
- Network with peers and future colleagues, and build bridges for potential research collaboration
- Interact with other researchers at the main EuroSPI conference sessions

1.3 EuroSPI 2008 Conference Committee

Over the past 15 years EuroSPI established an international committee of selected well known experts in SPI who have been willing to participate on the Scientific Programme Committee, Industry Advisory Committee and Organising Committee. For 2008 conference the relevant programme chairs and co-chairs are:

- General Chair   Richard Messnarz, ISCN, Austria
- Scientific co-chair   Rory O Connor, Dublin City University, Ireland
- Scientific co-chair   Nathan Baddoo, University of Hertfordshire, UK
- Scientific co-chair   Kari Smolander, Lappeenranta University of Technology, Finland
- Doctoral co-chair   Fergal McCaffery, Dundalk Institute of Technology, Ireland
- Doctoral co-chair   Rory O Connor, Dublin City University, Ireland
- Industrial co-chair   Risto Nevalainen FiSMA and STTF, Norway
- Industrial co-chair   Chair Stephan Goericke, ISQI, Germany
- Industrial co-chair   Jorn Johansen, DELTA, Denmark
- Industrial co-chair   Mads Christiansen, DELTA, Denmark
- Industrial co-chair   Nils Brede Moe, SINTEF, Norway
- Marketing Chair   Miklos Biro, Corvinus University of Budapest, Hungary
- Organizing Chair   Adrienne Clarke, ISCN, Ireland

2 DOCTORAL SYMPOSIUM PAPERS

This book contains seven papers by Ph.D. students who are at various stages in there research studies, from early stage exploratory and research problem formulation, to later stage research execution and theory formulation.

Padraig O'Leary's research is concerned with the area of SPI and SPL (software product lines). He outlines the issues surrounding product derivation practices from a software product line approach and proposes the development of a product derivation process framework for software product line organisations. This research work is developing a process framework that comprises important tasks product line stakeholders have to perform during product derivation. The framework is based on both literature and industrial practice.

Zádor Dániel Kelemen discusses the issues surrounding the development of a common meta-model for process-based quality approaches and methods. His initial goal is to develop a common meta-model for different software quality approaches and methods, with a focus on presenting the structure of six widespread quality approaches emphasizing the similarities amongst them. He attempts to understand the structure of quality approaches which convert textually described approaches into a graphical representation, proposing that a graphical representation could help supporting organizations in using multiple quality approaches and methods in the same time.

In his paper on the planning process, Kevin Logue focuses on handling uncertainty in cost and development time, in terms of assigning functionality to upcoming software releases. A task which can be difficult for even experienced software developers, who typically make decisions when required information is incomplete and/or unavailable. His research proposes a relatively simple statistical methodology that allows for uncertainty in both business value and cost to develop. It provides key stakeholders with the ability to determine the probability of completing a release on time and within budget. In addition, he outlines a case study conducted to demonstrate how the method may be used.

David Connolly's research is concerned with the concepts of the acceptance testing process and acceptance test driven development (ATDD) in particular. The ATDD process uses customer interaction to define tests and uses tool support to automate and execute these tests against system code. With existing tools, tests are usually written from customer descriptions or rewritten from existing documentation. David identifies a research challenge, which is to allow developers and customers to access this text, annotate it digitally and then produce valid Framework for Integrated Test (FIT) Tables. He proposes that ATDD can be enhanced by allowing tests to be created from existing documents and this can help in reducing the possibility of specifying tests incorrectly and of clarifying existing business rules.

Jean Carlo Rossa Hauck presents his PhD research proposal on the development of a process reference model for telemedicine software development. He proposes the analysis, development and evaluation of a tailored process reference model for the assessment and improvement of software development and maintenance of asynchronous web-based diagnostic telemedicine systems based on existing standards and reference models. His argument centres on the proposition that such a tailored reference model can facilitate SPI in the domain of telemedicine software development as well as contribute positively to the quality of the systems and services being developed.

Shuib Bin Basri discusses the related concepts of software process maintenance and evolution in the context of Irish software VSEs (Very Small Enterprises). In this paper he focuses on the issues of maintenance and evolution of Software Process in Irish Software companies and discusses how an organised knowledge process together with effective team development could influence software organisations in maintaining and evolving software process. His research method involves both qualitative and quantitative approaches. In addition he also proposes a model which will drive his Ph.D. research.

Namgyal Damdul proposes combining Interaction Design and Agile Methods to assist with improved project management in the domain of Internet development. In this paper, he identifies the problematic issues of managing large-scale internet projects using traditional software project management practices and the role of Agile Methods in this context. He identifies a research problem, which is to propose a systematic way of analyzing user groups and their expectations to enhance existing project management approaches within agile methods, particularly for the development of internet projects.

3 RECOMMENDED FURTHER READING

From the previous 14 years of EuroSPI conferences and its associated publications we highlight the following sources of EuroSPI associated SPI research literature. In Messnarz and Tully (1999) we integrated the proceedings of 3 EuroSPI conferences into one book which was edited by 30 experts in Europe.

The proceedings of the four most recent EuroSPI conferences have been published by Springer Verlag in the Lecture Notes in Computer Science series and are available as; Dingsøyr (2004), Richardson et al. (2005), Richardson et al. (2006) and Abrahamsson et al. (2007).

In addition selected best papers from the Industry Experience track of EuroSPI conferences are published each year by Wiley in the Journal of Software Process Improvement and Practice. In particular we would draw your attention to two recent issues published as Biró and Messnarz (2007) and Dingsøyr (2006).

References

Abrahamsson, P.; Baddoo, N.; Margaria, T.; Messnarz, R. (Eds.), *Software Process Improvement*, Lecture Notes in Computer Science , Vol. 4764, Springer Verlag, 2007

Biró, M. and Messnarz R., European industrial experiences in process improvement and innovation, *Software Process Improvement and Practice*, Vol. 12, No. 6, 2007

Dingsøyr, T, The European Software Process Improvement Conference, *Software Process Improvement and Practice*, Vol. 11, No. 1, 2006.

Dingsøyr, T. (Ed.), *Software Process Improvement*, Lecture Notes in Computer Science, Vol. 3281, Springer Verlag, 2004

Messnarz R., Tully C. (eds.), *Better Software Practice for Business Benefit - Principles and Experience*, IEEE Computer Society Press, September 1999

Richardson I., Abrahamsson P, Messnarz R., (Eds.), *Software Process Improvement*, Lecture Notes in Computer Science, Vol. 3792, Springer Verlag, 2005

Richardson, I., Runeson, P., Messnarz, R. (Eds.), *Software Process Improvement*, Lecture Notes in Computer Science, vol. 4257, Springer Verlag, 2006

DEVELOPING A PRODUCT DERIVATION PROCESS FRAMEWORK FOR SOFTWARE PRODUCT LINE ORGANISATIONS

Padraig O'Leary, Lero, The Irish Software Engineering Research Centre, University of Limerick, Limerick, Ireland, padraig.oleary@lero.ie

Ita Richardson, Lero, The Irish Software Engineering Research Centre, University of Limerick, Limerick, Ireland, ita.richardson@lero.ie

Steffen Thiel, Lero, The Irish Software Engineering Research Centre, University of Limerick, Limerick, Ireland, steffen.thiel@lero.ie

Abstract

Inefficient product derivation practices can greatly diminish the productivity gains expected from a software product line approach. As a foundation for systematic and efficient product derivation a better understanding of the underlying activities in industrial product line development is required.

This research has been developing a process framework that comprises important tasks product line stakeholders have to perform during product derivation. The framework is based on both literature and industrial practice. In this report, the status of the current research is presented along with the observations obtained thus far and how these observations were obtained.

Keywords: Software Product Lines, Product Derivation, process framework.

1 RESEARCH BACKGROUND

1.1 Research Question

Product derivation is a complex activity, involving a unique mesh of traditional software engineering approaches. However, product derivation practices are still at an early stage of evolution, and has primarily been driven by both industry and tool approaches to product derivation. In the absence of a theoretical approach to product derivation this research is focusing on the following research question:

"What are the basic activities in the product derivation process and to what extent can the development of a product derivation process framework guide organisations towards a "best-practice" approach to PD?"

1.2 Research Aims and Objectives

The main aims and objectives of this research project are to:

1. Develop a framework for the product derivation process that provides enhanced support for the derivation of products from a Software Product Line.

2. Validate the framework

1

1.3 Motivation for the Research

Product Derivation is the process of constructing a product from a Software Product Lines (SPL) core assets (Deelstra et al., 2005). An effective product derivation process can help to ensure that the effort required to develop the platform assets is less than the benefits delivered through using these shared artefacts across the products within a product line. In fact, the underlying assumption in SPL that "the investments required for building the reusable assets during domain engineering are outweighed by the benefits of rapid derivation of individual products" (Deelstra et al., 2004) might not hold if inefficient derivation practices diminishes the expected gains.

In the literature a number of publications speak of the difficulties associated with product derivation. Hotz et al. (Hotz et al., 2003) describe the process as "slow and error prone even if no new development is involved". Griss (Griss, 2000) identifies the inherent complexity and the coordination required in the derivation process by stating that "...as a product is defined by selecting a group of features, a carefully coordinated and complicated mixture of parts of different components are involved". Therefore as Deelstra (Deelstra et al., 2005) points out, the derivation of individual products from shared software assets is still a time-consuming and expensive activity in many organisations. Despite this, there has been little work dedicated to the overall product derivation process. Rabiser et al. (Rabiser et al., 2007) claim that "guidance and support are needed to increase efficiency and to deal with complexity of product derivation". Therefore as Deelstra (Deelstra et al., 2005) states there "is a lack of methodological support for application engineering and, consequently, organizations fail to exploit the full benefits of software product families."

2 LITERATURE REVIEW

2.1 Software Development Process Models

As SPL has its roots in general software engineering, research that specialises on SPL process models has to consider work on software engineering process models. As an example of these software engineering process models, the researcher is focusing on the on the Rational Unified Process (RUP) and agile methodologies.

Rational Unified Process. The Rational Unified Process (RUP) (Kruchten, 2004) provides a disciplined approach to the assignment of tasks and responsibilities within a process. RUP is supported by tools, which automate parts of the process. These tools are used to create and maintain the various artefacts of the process. RUP is a configurable process. It acknowledges that no single process is suitable for all software development projects. Hence, it provides a generalised process architecture that provides commonality across a family of processes and can be adapted for the particular case. RUP claims to have captured many of the best practices in modern software development in a form that is useful and suitable for a wide range of projects and organizations.

Agile Methodologies. Agile practices have recently gained popularity as a mechanism for reducing costs and increasing ability to handle change in dynamic market conditions. Researchers and practitioners have proposed several software development approaches based on the principles of the Agile manifesto . The Agile manifesto allows for changing requirements throughout the development cycle and stresses collaboration between developers and customers, and early product delivery. People (coupled with effectiveness and manoeuvrability) are considered the primary drivers of project success (Highsmith et al., 2001). eXtreme Programming (XP) and Scrum are two well-known agile practices based on the agile manifesto. XP emphasises technical aspects; while Scrum concentrates on project management.

2.2 Product Derivation Approaches and Tools

To date, several approaches and tools that support or partly automate product derivation activities in SPL have been proposed. Krebs et al. (Krebs et al., 2005) outline a derivation methodology that uses a configuration model to represent functionality and variability in a product line. The configuration model supports two types of artefacts: components and features. The components are derived from the physical architecture of the product line. Features represent a customer's view of the functionality in the components. A mapping between features and components allows for automated inferring of the components required for a given selection of features.

Asikainen et al. (Asikainen et al., 2004) provide a product configuration modelling language (PCML) and configuration tool (WeCoTin). PCML supports the creation of feature models for a software product line. WeCoTin is used to derive valid feature models for particular products of the product line.

The ConIPF Methodology (Hotz et al., 2003) proposed by Hotz et al. tackles the challenges of product derivation by combining concepts from product line engineering and knowledge-based configuration.

Rabiser et al. (Rabiser et al., 2007) present an approach for supporting product derivation using feature specifications. The approach introduces business decision-making into product derivation through a combination of modelling stakeholder needs, product features, architectural elements, and variability. The approach emphasises supporting the requirements acquisition and management mechanism through the use of variability models.

McGregor (Chastek et al., 2002) introduces the *production plan*, which prescribes how products are produced form platform assets. It contains the attached processes of the platform assets as well as an overall scheme of how the processes are combined to build products. The product plan facilitates the passing of knowledge between the platform developers and the product developers. A example of the production plan in use is given in (Chastek et al., 2002). McGregor (McGregor, 2005) also provides an overview of technologies and approaches to automate product derivation.

Deelstra et al. (Deelstra et al., 2005) present a product derivation approach developed based on two industrial case studies. The framework consists of two phases: an initial and an iteration phase. During the initial phase, a first product configuration is derived from the product line artefacts. The initial configuration is modified in a number of subsequent iterations during the iteration phase until the product sufficiently implements the imposed requirements. Requirements that cannot be accommodated by existing assets are handled by product-specific adaptation or reactive evolution. Parts of the derivation framework have been implemented in a research tool called COVAMOF (Sinnema et al., 2006), a variability modelling framework which purports to solve the product derivation problems associated with dependencies.

The work by Deelstra et al. presents a framework of terminology and concepts for product derivation. The framework focuses on product configuration and is a high level attempt at providing the methodological support that Deelstra et al. (Deelstra et al., 2004) agree is required for product derivation.

3 THEORITICAL BASIS FOR WORK

This research aspires to develop a Product Derivation Process Framework (PDPF). The framework builds on work done by Deelstra et. al (Deelstra et al., 2005). It identifies tasks, roles, artefacts and process flows within product derivation. A framework, as proposed here, provides benefits to both academia and industry.

For academia, the framework provides structure to the area under concern. Hence, it becomes easier place a particular research topic in context. There is historical evidence of certain fields achieving progress at the expense of others, through the establishment of a core, theoretical structure (Latour, 1988). As a roadmap, the framework points to areas of uncertainty and helps identify remaining challenges. Such a roadmap encourages the insertion of those pieces that may be missing, or the extra detail that may be needed for a particular purpose or group.

For industry, it is envisaged that the development of the framework will help the advancement of product derivation practices. It will assist organisations by providing a structured approach to product derivation, making the process more predictable and manageable. Moreover, this enables the integration of non-standard techniques such as agile practices, at appropriate times of the development process (O'Leary et al., 2007; O'Leary et al., 2007).

It can be argued that without some established process framework for product derivation, the applied practices will be motivated by technological solutions (e.g., available tools), rather than good practice. Standardisation of the development process around a methodology rather than a tool facilitates technology change. Tools can be interchanged more easily once seen to work within the bounds of the methodology. The framework can also support the development of these tool environments to make the derivation of products more efficient and effective.

4   RESEARCH DESIGN

This section presents the research approach used in this study.

4.1   Steps in achieving research objectives

The steps required to complete this research are as follows:
1. Create an initial PD Process framework (COMPLETE)
   * Perform an extensive literature review of PD practices within SPL.
   * Extrapolate from the literature an initial process framework for PD.
   * Through a series of organised iterative workshops with SPL experts and practitioners, the framework is refined and assessed.
2. Iterative Workshop Series (COMPLETE)
   * Series of workshops organised over four month period, with five participants attending twice a month
   * The framework was iteratively developed based on comments and feedback from participants
3. Perform Case Study Research (COMPLETE)
   * Review Case Study Company PD practices based on company documentation
   * Perform two day in-dept facilitated workshop study
   * Create a technical report on documented Case Study Company practices
   * Validate documented practices by emailing technical report to the Case Study Company.
   * Revise initial version of framework based on technical report.
4. Perform Expert Opinion Analysis (NOT-STARTED)
   * Design research instrument construction
   * Perform pilot study of research instrument
   * Establish selection of key SPL experts who are willing to participate in the analysis
   * Refine and assess framework based on feedback
   * Iteratively develop framework, until it meets certain pre-defined stop criteria.

4.2 Objective 1 – Development of the Framework

The framework is being developed in response to the absence of a defined "best-practice" approach to PD within current literature (Section 1.2). This research intends to rectify this gap in knowledge. It is a requirement that the framework would take into account the particular domain of operation. It is envisaged that this would lead to a more efficient productive derivation process and one which reflects better the investment made by the SPL organisation in the development of platform assets.

The framework described in this report (Section 5) is an output of the first three steps. In the development of this version of the framework an extensive literature review of, existing SPL whitepapers, PD papers and software process improvement (SPI) practices, was conducted. Evidence and feedback from SPL practitioners and researchers was collected from organised workshops and case study research into industrial product derivation practices was conducted.

The output of this research will be a PD process framework that supports an organisation engaged in PD. The framework will provide a structured approach to the development of a situational PD process, i.e. a process that takes into account the particular domain of operation, for instance systems development will have additional cross discipline coordination tasks. It is envisaged that the framework will improve the effectiveness and efficiency of the PD process within SPL organisations by forcing the adoption of the most essential PD practices for a particular domain

4.3 Objective 2 – Validation of the Framework

The researcher is looking at the practices and processes involved in the derivation of products from a SPL rather than any end product of the derivation process. Accordingly, qualitative methods are appropriate when the process is being studied rather than the product (Patton, 1987).

The study itself can be classified as applied research and more specifically, as constructive research. Järvinen (Järvinen, 2001) defines constructive research as typically involving the building of a new innovation based on existing (research) knowledge and new technical or organisational advancements. Furthermore, Järvinen suggests that constructive research also involves an evaluation of the innovation. According to Järvinen, in constructive research it is possible to accept a prototype or even a plan as a research outcome instead of a final product.

According to Hakim (Hakim, 1987) small samples of experts can be used to develop and test explanations. Previous studies have used small samples to gain expert feedback to evaluate and support model development. There are many successful examples where expert opinion has been used to validate models. For example, Lauesen and Vinter used expert opinion to identify techniques for requirement defects prevention (Lauesen et al., 2001). This research plans to emulate such studies in its research design.

5 RESEARCH METHODS

5.1 Literature Review

The preparatory stage of this research was conducted as a review of SPL literature focusing in particular on PD. As suggested by Cooper (Cooper, 1984), the literature review is aimed at defining the research topic's current state of knowledge. More specifically the research aimed to identify the fundamental practices of PD, to study the existing PD practices as well as to chart the available empirical evidence on the topic – scientific as well as anecdotal.

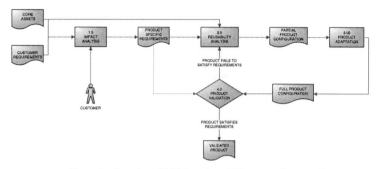

Figure 1 - Overview of initial version of PD process framework

The literature study undertook in this research revealed, among other issues, the lack of any defining methodological process for PD, and that PD approaches to date were centred on technological solutions that supported or partly automated the PD process. The output of the literature review was a first version of the PD process framework. The researcher organised the existing literature in PD and synthesised it to form the below framework (see Figure 1). This framework is validated theoretically through the use of existing literature from the SPL field. This theoretical validation can be seen in Chapter four through the use of theoretical arguments to support the various elements of the framework.

5.2 Iterative Workshop Series

The initial framework was further developed and assessed following organised workshops with SPL and SPI experts.

The participants were:
- An academic SPL expert
- An industrial SPL expert
- An academic software architecture expert
- An academic SPI and Agile expert
- The researcher of this study

This research defines 'expert' as a person who has either (a) published widely in recognised journals in the field of SPL and in particular PD; or (b) has practical experience of SPL – working in the field for several years and holding positions of responsibility.

The researcher organised a series of iterative workshops over a four months period, with participants meeting twice a month. Of the five participants, a minimum of three were present at each workshop. Prior to each workshop, the framework was sent to each participant, allowing them to familiarise themselves with the version being analysed. At each workshop an interactive presentation on the framework was given by the researcher. Issues requiring clarification or which where disputed among participants were discussed. Clarification and agreement was sought on varying issues through which the framework was further developed.

5.3 Case Study on Industrial Product Derivation Practices

The case study approach has always been one of the most popular research strategies (Orlikowski et al., 1991). The case study method is a powerful and flexible technique, considered suitable for exploratory research both prospectively and retrospectively (Perry et al., 2004). A case study is especially helpful in situations where researchers are seeking to develop understandings of the dynamics of a phenomenon in its natural context (Yin, 2003). As this study wished to investigate PD practices in industry the case study methodology seemed very applicable. In addition, previously, the researcher identified this study as an interpretive study (Section 3.6.1). Walsham (Walsham, 1993) stated that "case studies provide the main vehicle for research in the interpretive tradition".

For the case study, the researcher collected data on the PD process of a major supplier of automotive software. The company was implementing an SPL approach to software development. The researcher met the company where he presented a short presentation on the research project and the nature of the commitment required for any participant company.

For the case study, the researcher collected data on the product derivation practices of a major supplier of automotive systems. The systems produced consisted of both hardware (such as processors, sensors, connectors, and housing) and software. Many of the requirements were derived from market segments, such as low cost or high cost customers or from regulatory requirements.

According to Yin (Yin, 2003), the use of multiple sources of evidence in a case study allows an investigator to address a broader range of historical, attitudinal, and behavioural issues. Furthermore, the multiple sources of empirical evidence provide an opportunity for triangulation in order to make any finding or conclusion of the study more convincing and accurate (Yin, 2003). Yin identifies six sources of evidence: documentation, archival records, interviews, direct-observation, participant-observation, and physical artefacts (Yin, 2003).

While conducting the case study the researcher had access the following sources of evidence:
- Company documentation
- Collective group notes from workshop
- Whiteboard drawings of company practices collected from workshop
- Researcher notes of workshop discussion

After the workshop the collected data is used to create a technical report on the company derivation practices. This technical report is currently being compiled. On completion the report will be sent to the company for validation.

5.4 Expert Opinion Assessment

The researcher plans to target key SPL experts' world wide to participate in the study. The researcher will choose experts from different backgrounds and audiences groups as recommended by Lauesen and Vinter (Lauesen et al., 2001) and Kitchenham et al. (Kitchenham et al., 2002). The researcher will aim to draw experts from both research and industry. Industry participants will be selected based on relativity, in terms of area, and their domain of expertise.

Expert opinion based assessments will be conducted through Delphi analysis, focus groups or questionnaires. With the arrival of SPLC'08 at the University of Limerick in September 08, the researcher would have a unique opportunity as the main SPL experts in the world would be visiting the university. This provides an opportunity to engage SPL experts face to face who, perhaps for geographical reasons, would typically be inaccessible for this study.

The researcher is currently constructing a list of willing participants for the assessment. Once confirmation and final numbers of willing participants is received, meeting schedules will be organised. Parallel to this, the researcher is investigating expert opinion assessment techniques for the purpose of conducting the assessment.

Feedback from the assessment would be used to refine and assess the framework.

6 RESULTS TO DATE

6.1 A Product Derivation Process Framework

The PDPF is structured into four main steps:

1 **Impact Analysis** is aimed at gathering product-specific requirements based on customer requirements and negotiation with the platform team.
2 **Reusability Analysis** purports to create a partial product configuration based on the product specific requirements and by using the available core assets.
3 During **Component Development and Adaptation**, new components are developed (if required) and existing components are adapted to satisfy requirements which could not be satisfied by configuring existing core assets.
4 Finally, **Product Integration and Validation** aims to integrate the core asset configuration and newly developed components. The integrated product is then validated by performing appropriate testing procedures.

The researcher will now discuss these product derivation steps in more detail.

6.2 Formalising the framework

The researcher is using the Eclipse Process Framework (EPF) to model the product derivation process and create a more formal version of the PDPF. EPF allows the development, maintenance and deployment of process content. It also allows the development of situational method content. By enabling inbuilt process variability within EPF you can select, tailor and or remove content from a process in order to strike the right balance for a particular situation. This has the potential for making the PDPF as applicable to a small software development team working on a mobile application as it is for large aerospace and defence contractor building a system of systems. For instance, in the case study company the researcher saw that embedded software development is a cross discipline activity. In this context, discipline mapping where requirements are allocated to software, hardware or mechanical disciplines, would be a relevant task. However discipline mapping might be different when developing a product line in another domain. This process flexibility allows the researcher to model generic product derivation practices and domain specific practices.

Figure 2. New Tasks in Impact Analysis

7 CONCLUSION AND FUTURE WORK

This research is motivated by the assumption that despite the adoption of SPL within industry, product derivation remains an expensive and error-prone activity.

The researcher has presented a product derivation framework which is based on an extensive literature review and discussions with SPL practitioners and researchers. The researcher studied the product derivation practices of a large automotive supplier. The observations from this case study research resulted in augmentations for our framework, especially for industries which focus on software-intensive systems (which include other aspects besides software).

The researcher hope the framework will assist organisations in applying a structured approach to product derivation activities. To progress towards that aspiration the researcher sees a multitude of potential research avenues.

The researcher's goal for the near future is to provide a version of the PDPF which is completely described electronically, i.e. in models used by the Eclipse Process Framework (EPF). First, this would allow easy access to documentation and guidelines, since these models can be published as a website. Second, it allows the researcher to employ variability in the process framework. Consequently, the models can be adapted and customized for a particular industry and organization. This is adaptation is already tool- supported by EPF Composer (The Eclipse Foundation, 2007).

In the long run, the framework itself could be used as a foundation for tools, which support the process side of product derivation. This could include support for process management, for instance, by increasing the visibility of status information on tasks, milestones and key deliverables.

To gather meaningful information with minimal additional effort, it would be desirable to integrate the PDPF tools with existing practices. For instance, the tool could detect the current tasks and artefacts the developer is working on, by interaction (hotkeys) or by analysing access operations to a version control server. Integrated with the status overview (of tasks and artefacts) the tool could provide functionality to start task-specific activities or jump directly to an artefact.

As a further aspect of the product derivation processes, the researcher is interested in the integration of agile practices with plan-driven approaches. The researcher believes that in many contexts the adoption of agile practices can improve the product derivation process. The researchers work to date in this area has identified a set of agile practices that have potential for integration into the product derivation process (O'Leary et al., 2007; O'Leary et al., 2007). The researcher believes that our framework can provide a means to balancing between agility and formalism during the product derivation process.

References

The Eclipse Foundation. Eclipse Process Framework Project (EPF) Available on-line from: http://www.eclipse.org/epf, Accessed November 29th 2007.

Asikainen, T., T. Männistö, et al. (2004). Using a Configurator for Modelling and Configuring Software Product Lines Based on Feature Models. 3rd Software Product Line Conference (SPLC 2004). Boston, MA,.

Chastek, G., P. Donohoe, et al. (2002). Product Line Production Planning for the Home Integration System Example. Product Line Practice Initiative. Pittsburgh, Software Engineering Institute.

Chastek, G. and J. D. McGregor (2002). Guidelines for Developing a Product Line Production Plan. Product Line Practice Initiative. Pittsburgh, PA, Software Engineering Institute.

Cooper, H. M. (1984). The Integrative Research Review: A Systematic Approach. Beverly Hills, Sage Publications, Inc.

Deelstra, S., M. Sinnema, et al. (2004). Experiences in Software Product Families: Problems and Issues During Product Derivation. Software Product Lines, Third International Conference. Boston, MA, USA, Springer.

Deelstra, S., M. Sinnema, et al. (2005). Product Derivation in Software Product Families: A Case Study. J. Syst. Softw. New York, NY, USA, Elsevier Science Inc. 74: 173-194.

Griss, M. L. (2000). Implementing Product-Line Features with Component Reuse. London, UK, Springer-Verlag.

Hakim, C. (1987). Research design : strategies and choices in the design of social research. London, Allen & Unwin.

Highsmith, J. and A. Cockburn (2001). Agile Software Development: The Business of Innovation. IEEE Computer. 34: 120-122.

Hotz, L., A. Gunter, et al. (2003). A Knowledge-based Product Derivation Process and some Ideas how to Integrate Product Development. Proc. of Software Variability Management Workshop. Groningen, The Netherlands.

Järvinen, P. (2001). On Research Methods. Tampere, Finland, Juvenes-Print.

Kitchenham, B., S. Pfleeger, et al. (2002). "Preliminary guidelines for empirical research in software engineering." IEEE Transactions on Software Engineering 28(8): 721 - 734.

Krebs, T., K. Wolter, et al. (2005). Model-based Configuration Support for Product Derivation in Software Product Families. Koblenz, Germany.

Kruchten, P. (2004). The Rational Unified Process: An Introduction, Addison-Wesley.

Latour, B. (1988). The Pasteurization of France. Cambridge, MA, Harvard University Press.

Lauesen, S. and O. Vinter (2001). "Preventing Requirement Defects: an Experiment in Process Improvement." Requirements Engineering Journal 6(1): 37-50.

McGregor, J. D. (2005). Preparing for Automated Derivation of Products in a Software Product Line, Software Engineering Institute,.

O'Leary, P., M. Ali Babar, et al. (2007). Product Derivation Process and Agile Approaches: Exploring the Integration Potential. Proceedings of 2nd IFIP Central and East European Conference on Software Engineering Techniques, Poznań, Poland, Wydawnictwo NAKOM.

O'Leary, P., M. Ali Babar, et al. (2007). Towards Agile Product Derivation in Software Product Line Engineering. RISE 2007, 4th International Workshop on Rapid Integration of Software Engineering techniques, Luxembourg, LUXEMBOURG.

Orlikowski, W. and J. Baroudi (1991). "Studying Information Technology in Organizations: Research Approaches and Assumptions." Information Systems Research.

Patton, M. Q. (1987). How to Use Qualitative Methods in Evaluation. California, Sage Publications Inc.

Perry, D., S. E. Sim, et al. (2004). Case Studies for Software Engineers. Proceedings of the 26th International Conference on Software Engineering.

Rabiser, R., P. Grunbacher, et al. (2007). Supporting Product Derivation by Adapting and Augmenting Variability Models. Software Product Line Conference, 2007. SPLC 2007. 11th International. Kyoto, Japan.

Sinnema, M., S. Deelstra, et al. (2006). Modeling Dependencies in Product Families with COVAMOF. 13th Annual IEEE International Conference and Workshop on the Engineering of Computer Based Systems (ECBS 2006). Potsdam, Germany.

Walsham, G. (1993). Interpreting Information Systems in Organizations. New York, NY, USA, John Wiley & Sons, Inc.

Yin, R. K. (2003). Case Study Research: Design and Methods. Thousand Oaks, CA, Sage Publications Inc.

STRUCTURE OF PROCESS-BASED QUALITY APPROACHES -ELEMENTS OF A RESEARCH DEVELOPING A COMMON META-MODEL FOR PROCESS-BASED QUALITY APPROACHES AND METHODS

Zádor Dániel Kelemen, Department of Control Engineering and Information Technology, Budapest University of Technology and Economics, Budapest, Hungary, kelemen.daniel@sqi.hu

Katalin Balla, Department of Control Engineering and Information Technology, Budapest University of Technology and Economics, Budapest, Hungary, balla@iit.bme.hu

Jos Trienekens, Department of Technology Management, Eindhoven University of Technology, The Netherlands, J.J.M.Trienekens@tue.nl

Rob Kusters, Department of Technology Management, Eindhoven University of Technology, The Netherlands, R.J.Kusters@tue.nl

Abstract

The paper describes the basic idea and the first steps of a PhD research program, having the goal to develop a common meta-model for different software quality approaches and methods. At this time, we focus on presenting the structure of 6 widespread quality approaches emphasizing the similarities amongst them. Understanding the structure of quality approaches helps converting textually described approaches into graphical representation. A graphical representation could help supporting organizations in using multiple quality approaches and methods in the same time.

Keywords: Software Process Improvement, CMMI, ISO 9001:2000, modeling quality approaches, structure of quality approaches.

1 INTRODUCTION

Several quality methods, standards and models have been developed in the last few decades to guide software developing organizations in defining and institutionalizing their processes. These approaches are essential in improving the company's own quality system, but each of them uses an own view on quality.

However, software companies (want to / are forced to) use more quality approaches simultaneously, they often struggle with interpreting them, due to different terminology and their different point of view on quality.

In the day-by-day consultancy work, we experienced that software companies often implement quality approaches separately, without unifying or harmonizing the common elements. Problems connected to process interpretation and implementation usually come when companies have separated process descriptions for different quality approaches and methods. In this case, project managers have to choose between approaches. Due to the different standards, projects are focusing in different ways on quality. Some (eg. ISO 9001:2000) projects are focusing on measurement of customer satisfaction and customer relationship management but not on technical solution and product integration. Others (eg. in CMMI-based projects) may concentrate on requirements development, management and traceability, but not on handling the customer's property.

The situation may become more complicated, when the processes built on different quality approaches include different descriptions of same areas (eg. change management or measurement).

Our work has the scope to give a solution to the problem described: defining a meta-model would be useful to harmonize the quality-related concepts from different approaches.

The PhD research program planned for 4 years (2007-2010) has the following main steps:
- comparing elements of selected quality approaches;
- selecting the possible main elements to be used for the meta-model;
- examining the content and structure quality approaches and methods;
- examining quality of transformations, especially information loss during transformations;
- research in the field of enterprise modelling and selecting the useful concepts of the field;
- developing the first version of the methodology/meta-model and testing it at Hungarian and Dutch companies;
- refinements on the meta-model, based on practical results, developing final version.

The meta-model would make use of elements found to be common in more quality approaches, structuring them in a way that would be acceptable in connection with more quality approaches.

In the first phase of our research we focused on studying modelling techniques and on understanding basic elements of well known quality approaches and methods, in order to be able to choose the common elements that would form the basis of the meta-model. Here we present results of our investigation.

In order to model the quality approaches, we considered important to know the elements and structure of them, therefore *our research question was the following: What are the elements of quality approaches?*

We provide brief literature reviews connected to different steps of the research at the beginning of chapters 2, 3 and 5.

Chapter 2 of this paper summarises the process modelling evolution, based on G. Cugola's and C. Ghezzi's point of view. In chapter 3 we present our research aspects. Afterwards (in chapter 4) we describe the base structure of the most used (software) quality approaches (as ISO 9001:2000, ISO 9004:2000, ISO 90003:2004, CMMI-DEV v1.2, ISO-IEC 12207-95 and ISO-IEC 15939-2002). We show a comparison of the elements of quality approaches mentioned with the elements of a process. In chapter 5 we present the application of modelling process to Nelson and Monarchi quality modelling framework. Finally, in chapter 6 we present an idea for harmonising common areas of quality approaches. We conclude by presenting a summary of the results obtained in exploring the structure of quality approaches.

2   PROCESS MODELLING

In "Software Processes: a Retrospective and a Path to the Future" Cugola et al. (1998) have shown (table 1.) the main steps of software process evolution starting from the early 60's. In table 1 strengths and weaknesses of lifecycle models, methodologies, formal development, automation, management and improvement are shown.

After these approaches, a new era came for processes: process modelling and process programming. In process modelling there are several research works, like Process Modelling Languages (PML) –introduced by Osterweil (1987), Little JIL process modelling language

(Osterweil (2007)), Oz Web – the first "decentralized" PSEE was developed at Columbia University., Endeavors, BPM or enterprise modelling Wortmann et al. (2007).

#	Name	Examples	Strength	Weakness
1.	Lifecycle models	Waterfall model	Well structured, clear documentation	Idealised processes
2.	Methodologies	Jackson System Development (JSD), JSP	Based on experiences from previous projects	Informal notation, increased paperwork
3.	Formal development	Program development by stepwise refinement	Transforms specification to correct implementation	Not scalable, applicable only for small programs
4.	Automation	Software Development Environments (SDEs)	Automation of some areas of software production	Requirements specification, design decisions cannot be automated
5.	Management & improvement	ISO9001: 2000, CMMI, TSP, PSP	Indirect assurance of quality products	Increased bureaucracy

Table 1. – Evolution of software processes

Process modelling can be classified in several ways, eg. by architectures and modelling approaches.

The minimalist process modelling approach describes only the most important elements of processes, and it is easily understandable for people. The maximalist approach describes and validates the whole process model. Processes built in maximalist way can be processed by computers, but are more difficult to understand by humans.

From the architectural point of view top-down process approaches start from the idea to the implementation, bottom-up approaches try to model the manifested processes.

We have chosen the following goal in the Ph.D work: to understand the structure of the process based quality approaches, and create a common meta-model in a minimalist way, which will be easily understandable for quality managers and project managers. Using this meta-model, processes could be built in a top-down or a bottom-up way.

3   RESEARCH METHODOLOGY

At the beginning of the work, our goal was to have practically useful results; therefore the following two aspects were considered important:
1. to analyse the structure of the *widespread approaches*,
2. to *describe the structure* of approaches analysed in a very *simple* and understandable *format*.

In order to satisfy the goal 1, in the project IKKK-GVOP-2004-3.2.2 we analysed the actual situation of software processes having table 1. in mind (IKKK 2008). Major Hungarian software companies were surveyed about their processes and development methodologies. We came to the conclusion that nowadays, management and improvement approaches are widely used. In the following, we concentrate on quality approaches focusing on management and improvement of software processes.

Process-based quality approaches are often textually described, and in order to model them we need to know what their basic elements are.

In Hungary, the most used and "mandatory" quality approach is ISO 9001:2000 - Quality management systems – requirements. At present 439 IT-related companies are ISO 9001:2000

13

certified. See IMCC (2008) for the list of ISO 9001:2000 certified Hungarian software companies. Besides ISO 9001:2000, most used approaches are the Capability Maturity Model Integration (CMMI) and (Automotive) SPICE (Software Process Improvement and Capability dEtermination, also known as ISO/IEC 15504). While software companies use CMMI, suppliers of multinational car factories prefer Automotive SPICE as a second approach.

Further well-known standards connected to software processes are ISO 9004:2000, ISO 90003:2004, ISO-IEC 12207-95 and ISO-IEC 15939-2002.

Knowing what quality approaches companies are using, we selected the next approaches:
- CMMI for Development, Version 1.2
- ISO 9001:2000 Quality management systems – requirements
- ISO 9004:2000 Quality management systems – Guidelines for performance improvements
- ISO/IEC 90003:2000 Software Engineering – Guidelines for the application of ISO9001:2000 to computer software
- ISO/IEC 15939-2002 – "Information technology - Software measurement process"
- ISO/IEC 12207-95 – "Information technology - Software life cycle process"

Having in mind our second research aspect, we chose UML class diagrams for describe the structure of quality approaches. However, the approaches analysed could be described in several ways in UML class diagrams, to keep the simplicity, we used only the aggregation relationship between the elements.

4   STRUCURE OF QUALITY APPROACHES

In this chapter we briefly present the structure of quality approaches selected in the previous chapter.

ISO 9001:2000 is an international standard which contains general requirements for quality management systems (QMS). The requirements included in this standard are so general that can be applied at any company.

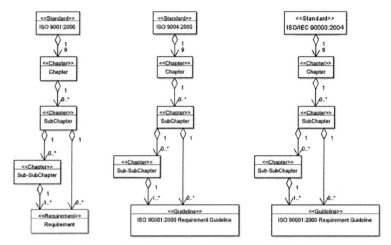

Fig. 1 - The Structure of ISO 9001:2000, ISO 9004:2000 and ISO/IEC 90003:2000

Looking at this standard, we can see that it contains 9 chapters, which could contain subchapters and the subchapters also can contain further subchapters. Requirements of this quality approach can be found at subchapter and sub-subchapter level in sentences. Figure 1. shows the structure of ISO 9001:2000 and two, other ISO 9001:2000-connected standards.

The structure of ISO 9004:2000 "Quality management systems – Guidelines for performance improvements" and ISO/IEC 90003:2000 "Software Engineering – Guidelines for the application of ISO9001:2000 to computer software" are identical to ISO 9001:2000 because these are using ISO 9001:2000 as a basis, containing the same chapters. The only difference amongst them is that the latter two define guidelines instead of focusing on requirements.

As we already mentioned, other two widespread approaches are CMMI and SPICE. CMMI is an integrated model, it integrates ideas from CMM, SPICE and further international quality standards, therefore most of the requirements of the SPICE model can be derived from CMMI. Here we focus on CMMI.

The actual version of CMMI, v1.2 defines 3 constellations: CMMI for Development, CMMI for Acquisition and CMMI for Services. Different constellations include different sets of process areas of the model. Looking at its structure, the model contains required, expected and informative components. Informative components are guidelines, specific and generic practices are the concrete, expected requirements. Required components are derived from expected components. A CMMI practice is considered performed if there are enough evidences and affirmations available to prove the accomplishment, a goal is achieved if all the connected practices are performed, a process is implemented when all its goals are achieved. For more details see SCAMPI (2008).

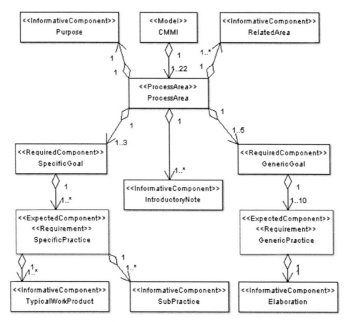

Fig. 2. - The Structure of CMMI-DEV v1.2

Standard ISO/IEC 15939-2002 – "Information technology - Software measurement process" defines process activities and sub activities required for the measurement process.

ISO/IEC 12207-95 – "Information technology - Software life cycle process" describes processes, activities, tasks, entry and exit conditions, responsibilities and documentation requirements for software lifecycle processes.

In this chapter have shown the structure of 6 different quality approaches. In each of them we found the elements *requirements* or *guidelines*. In ISO standards, requirements and guidelines are usually textually described, in sentences. In other approaches, like CMM, CMMI or SPICE different levels and categories of requirements can be found.

We started to analyse further approaches and methods like Agile methods and IT Infrastructure Library (ITIL) and we made similar observations.

We found in the presented 6 approaches several types of elements: eg. chapter, requirements, guidelines, process, process description, activity, process activity, activity description, task, option, entry and exit condition, documentation requirement, responsibility, process area, specific and generic goal, specific and generic practice, typical work product, subpractice, practice elaboration etc.

It is generally accepted by the software community that software processes are described by using the elements: *inputs, activities, outputs,* purpose, entry and exit criteria, roles, measures, and verification steps (see SEI (2006)). We considered the same elements as starting point for our disquisition and compared them to elements commonly used by software quality models.

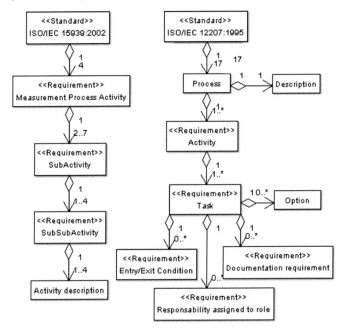

Fig. 3. - The Structure of ISO/IEC 15939-2002 and ISO/IEC 12207-95

We found several coincidences amongst elements of quality approaches and process elements. Process, process description, activity, process activity, activity description and task are proportional to the *activity* element of processes. Documentation requirements and typical work products are proportional are similar to *inputs* and *outputs*.

We found software quality model - element types which have no similarities to process elements. Such elements are eg. benefits, critical success factors, features or key performance indicators in ITIL.

Obviously, in order to model textual descriptions, it is not enough to analyse the structure, it is also important to know the content (fig. 4.). A content-based quality framework (Balla et al. (2001)) and support tool (Kelemen et al. (2007)) was already developed showing the objects and quality aspects of different quality approaches. We also consider important researches exploring the differences and similarities amongst quality approaches regarding the content, terminology, ROI etc. (Balla et al. (2001), Kelemen et al. (2008a)).

5 QUALITY OF MODELLING PROCESS

Exploring the structure of different process-based quality approaches and methods is just one step in transforming the textually described models to a more understandable and shorter graphical representation. Important question is how the quality of transformation can be assured?

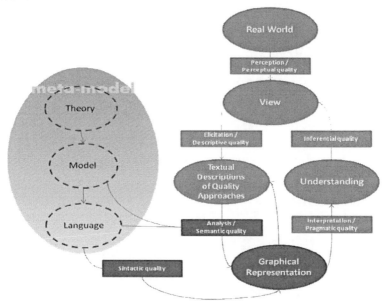

Fig. 4. – The quality approach modelling process in Nelson and Monarchi quality evaluation framework

However, the research area dealing with the quality of modelling process is still evolving (Nelson et al. (2007)), there are modelling frameworks already available. Such frameworks are the Lindland et al. (1994) framework (a recent revision in Krogstie et al. (2006)), the Wand and Wang framework (Wand et al. 1996) and Nelson's and Monarchi's model quality evaluation framework (Nelson et al. (2007)). These frameworks are concentrating on different objects and transformations, define several types of quality such as perceptual, descriptive, semantic, syntactic, pragmatic, inferential, physical, knowledge, tool, social or empirical quality.

Two main metrics of quality of modelling are completeness and validity. If B (the result of transformation) is missing some components that are present in A (the source of transformation) then B is incomplete (Nelson et al. (2007)). If the perception, elicitation, analysis and interpretation are complete and valid, there is a confidence that the overall method is complete and valid (Nelson et al. (2007)).

Nelson and Monarchi framework is known as the most recent from these all, it uses concepts from the other two frameworks.

In Nelson and Monarchi framework there are the following basic objects and transformations:
- Objects: The real world, View, Description, Representation, Understanding
- Transformations: Perception, Elicitation, Analysis, Interpretation, Implementation
- Analysis objects: Theory, Model, Language

If we use the Nelson and Monarchi framework in our modelling process besides developing a qualitative meta-model we need to focus on the semantic and syntactic quality in order to achieve a qualitative graphical representation. Pragmatic and inferential qualities are also important, because without these we cannot be sure that the user understands and forms the same view as the descriptor. In our point of view, perceptual and descriptive qualities are not so important because we already have the textual description of quality approaches.

6 CONCLUSION

In conclusion we can state that the idea to build a common meta-model for making the harmonisation of different of quality approaches and methods easier, seems both useful (as we emphasized in chapter 1) and feasible (chapter 2, 3).

In the first chapter we summarised the problems of simultaneously using multiple software quality models and standards. Modelling these approaches could provide a solution for the problems mentioned (as shown in chapter 2.). Process modelling architectures, approaches and modelling languages are available, which could serve a basis for the meta-model, some of them were mentioned.

Analysing the content of quality approaches we found that several approaches are focusing on the same problems (eg. change management can be found CMMI, ISO 9001:2000 and ITIL), but from different quality point of view.

Certainly, it is not enough to know the content of quality approaches, it is advisable to analyse their structure as well. Knowing the structure of quality approaches could serve a strong basis in identifying the main elements of the meta-model. Therefore, in chapter 4. we have shown the structure of 6 different quality approaches. Common elements were identified, examples of similarities and differences to process elements were shown.

We consider important to discover which parts of textual approaches can be modelled, and what are the elements/parts that cannot. In all the transformations the quality of modelling process must be assured. Some ideas connected to this subject were presented in chapter 5.

The way towards such a meta-model to model process-descriptive quality approaches requires further steps. We plan to continue the research with the following steps:
- analysing the structure and content further well-known quality approaches and methods;

- having discovered the main elements of quality approaches, selecting the possible main elements to be used for the meta-model;
- analysing process modelling languages, models and methods.
- examining information loss during transformations.

7 ACKNOWLEDGEMENT

This project has been supported by BME (IT)[2] (BME Innovation and Knowledge Centre of Information Technology) within the frame of Peter Pázmány Programme, National Office for Research and Technology, Hungary.

References

Automotive SPICE™ Process Assessment Model (PAM) RELEASE v2.3 (2007) http://www.automotivespice.com/web/download.html

Automotive SPICE™ Process Reference Model (PRM) RELEASE v4.3 (2007) http://www.automotivespice.com/web/download.html

Balla K., Bemelmans T., Kusters R., Trienekens J. J. M . (2001) "QMIM - Quality through Managed Improvement and Measurement". In Proceedings of European Software Control and Metrics Conference, London , pp. 315-326

Cugola, G. and Ghezzi, C. (1998), "Software Processes: a Retrospective and a Path to the Future" in Software Process: Improvement and Practice, Volume 4, Issue 3

IKKK-GVOP-2004-3.2.2 project webpage (2008) http://ikkk.inf.elte.hu/

ISO 9001:2000 Quality management systems – requirements

ISO 9004:2000 Quality management systems – Guidelines for performance improvements

ISO/IEC 90003:2000 Software Engineering – Guidelines for the application of ISO9001:2000 to computer software

ISO/IEC 15504-4:2004 Information technology -- Process assessment -- Part 4: Guidance on use for process improvement and process capability determination (SPICE)

ISO/IEC 15939-2002 – "Information technology - Software measurement process"

ISO/IEC 12207-95 – "Information technology - Software life cycle process"

IMCC - ISO Minősített Cégek címjegyzéke (List of ISO Qualified Hungarian Companies), (2008) http://www.imcc.hu/

Kelemen Z. D., Balla K. (2008a) „Comparing CMMI-DEV v1.2 and ISO 9001:2000", article in Hungarian Quality pp. 6 (in hungarian)

Kelemen Z. D., Balla K., Trienekens J., Kusters R. (2008b) „Towards Supporting Simultaneous Use of Process-based Quality Approaches", in Conference Proceedings of ICCC 2008, paper id: 69

Kelemen Z. D., Balla K., Bóka G. (2007): "Quality Organizer: a support tool in using multiple quality approaches", in Conference Proceedings of ICCC 2007, pp. 280-285

Krogstie J., Sindre G. and Jørgensen H. (2006), "Process models representing knowledge for action: a revised quality framework", European Journal of Information Systems 15, 91–102

Lindland, O.I., Sindre, G., Solvberg, A. (1994), Understanding quality in conceptual modeling. IEEE Software 11(2):42–49.

Nelson H. J. and Monarchi D. E. (2007), "Ensuring the quality of conceptual representations", in Software Quality Journal 15:213-233

Osterweil, L. (1987), "Software Processes are Software too", in Proceedings of the Ninth International Conference on Software Engineering.

Osterweil, L. (2007), "What We Learn from the Study of Ubiquitous Processes" Software Process: Improvement and Practice, Volume 12, Issue 5 pp. 399 - 414

Software Engineering Institute (2006) - Standard CMMI Appraisal Method for Process Improvement webpage - http://www.sei.cmu.edu/cmmi/appraisals/

Software Engineering Institute (1993) - Capability Maturity Model for Software (CMM) http://www.sei.cmu.edu/cmm/

Software Engineering Institute (2006), – "CMMI for Development, Version 1.2" http://www.sei.cmu.edu/publications/documents/06.reports/06tr008.html

UML (2008), Object Management Group's Unified Modeling Language webpage http://www.uml.org/

Wand, Y., Wang, R. (1996), "Anchoring data quality dimensions in ontological foundations", in Communications of the ACM 39(11): pp. 86–95.

Wortmann, H., Kusters, R. (2007), book "Enterprise Modelling and Enterprise Information Systems"

THE PLANNING PROCESS: HANDLING UNCERTAINTY IN COST AND DEVELOPMENT TIME

Kevin Logue, Software Technology Research Centre, Dundalk Institute of Technology, Ireland, Kevin.Logue@dkit.ie

Kevin McDaid, Department of Computing, Dundalk Institute of Technology, Ireland, Kevin.McDaid@dkit.ie

Abstract

The task of assigning functionality to upcoming releases can be difficult for even the most veteran software developers. Decisions are typically made when required information is incomplete and/or unavailable. This paper proposes a relatively simple statistical methodology that allows for uncertainty in both business value and cost to develop. In so doing it provides key stakeholders the ability to determine the probability of completing a release on time and to budget. The technique is lightweight in nature and consistent with existing agile planning practices. A case study is provided to demonstrate how the method may be used.

Keywords: Release Planning, Uncertainty, Agile Methodology.

1 INTRODUCTION

Studies as recent as 2004, have shown that a considerable number of software development projects suffer from cost or schedule overruns (Johnson, 2006). Reasons for this include unrealistic goals, inaccurate estimates, an ill-defined system, poor monitoring of project status and poor project management (Charette, 2008). Through the implementation of an honest and reliable release plan the chance of completing a project within the allocated time and budget can increase considerably (Cohn, 2006)

The task of selecting what functionality to complete in upcoming software releases is a complex process (Regnell & Brinkkemper, 2005). Typically a development has a finite amount of resources available, forcing developers to prioritize certain requirements to determent of others. The question of which stories to prioritize requires considerable understanding of both the technical complexity of the project and also a keen understanding of the product's market.

Little (Little, 2005) identifies four major areas of uncertainty that affect a software development project; market uncertainty, technical uncertainty, project duration and project dependencies. Market uncertainty relates to the understanding of customers' needs. Attempting to satisfy a smaller client base offers considerable less uncertainty, as developers can more easily prioritize desired requirements. Technical uncertainty occurs where the technical needs are not fully understood. Typically, technical uncertainty arises when using a new technology or when a problem is not well defined. The duration of a project is a major contributing factor to uncertainty. The more time required to complete a project the more likely that either market or technical uncertainties may arise. Project dependencies refer to the flexibility of a project, and in the event that one part of the project must be completed before another part starts the project's ability to absorb the occurrence of uncertain events diminishes.

This paper proposes a relatively simple statistical methodology designed to help developers to determine the likely completion time for a plan and its expected business value. The method recognises uncertainty in business value, required effort and resources available to develop a software project. The method is demonstrated and investigated through a case study.

The paper is structured as follows. Section 2 discusses related work in the area of release planning, requirement prioritisation and project uncertainty. Section 3 provides a brief overview of the methodology. Section 4 describes how the methodology can fit within a development process. Section 5 discusses how the methodology handles uncertainty. Section 6 demonstrates the methodology through a case study. Section 7 concludes this paper and outlines the future potential of the method.

2 RELATED WORK

The planning methodology proposed herein expands upon Extreme Programming's "Planning Game". The aim of the Planning Game is to select which requirements, in XP called user stories, to include in the next and upcoming releases. The process begins by first eliciting all requirements and expressing them in terms of a user story. A user story is a representation of a requirement written in a high level form free of technical jargon. Once all user stories have been gathered the team is asked to provide estimates of the size of each story in terms of ideal development days or story points. The size of the story in ideal development days represents the length of time it would take a developer to complete a story assuming that they are in a position to engage solely in the development activity. A story point on the other hand is an amalgamation of the size of task, its complexity and also its risk (Cohn, 2006). Next, the team attempts to prioritise user requirements. This prioritisation requires the development team to conduct a complex cost-benefit analysis to determine which stories offer maximum overall benefit.

Even when ignoring the issue of uncertainty, requirement prioritisation requires considerable time and effort on the part of the decision maker. Prioritisation techniques can be split into two categories, absolute and relative priority (Karlsson et al., 2007). An absolute technique assigns a priority to each requirement based upon its importance to the project. A well known example is the MoSCoW (Cohn, 2006) prioritisation technique which separates requirements into "must have", "should have", "could have" and "would like to" have sub groups. On the other hand, relative priority expresses each requirement with its own priority value. One such technique is the "Cost-Value" approach (Karlsson & Ryan, 1997). This approach compares all possible pairs of requirements, in order to determine which requirement is of higher priority. However while conceptually simple the method does not offer a simple means for developers to compare stories and as such does not guarantee maximum value for minimum cost (Jung, 1998).

Another method is the EVOLVE (Greer & Ruhe, 2004) approach. This approach takes into account stakeholder priorities, requirement constraints and also effort limits. On the face of it this method is quite suitable for agile planning, but requires the coordination of stakeholders in prioritizing requirements and a trust in that judgement. Further, the effort estimation is based on requirements and not explicitly on the constituent tasks that deliver those requirements. Given that user stories are a common vehicle for representing user requirements in agile approaches and that these tend to be at a high level, estimation is more suitable after the tasks involved have been identified.

An approach similar to that proposed within this paper is the Fuzzy Effort Constraint method (Ngo-The et al., 2004). This method acknowledges the issues with the provision of precise crisp estimates in the early stages of a project. Instead the development team is asked to provide minimum, maximum and most likely values to allow assuming estimates take the form of fuzzy triangular numbers. Once these estimates are in hand the method compares the required resources with the resources that are available to the project using a probabilistic approach. This comparison yields a measure of the degree to which the resource constraint has been met. In so doing it provides the decision makers with a series of possible plans with varying degrees of satisfaction and the level to which the resource constraint has been met. However the use of fuzzy numbers can make it unclear as to which solution is optimal. It can be difficult to apply a real world analogy to the concept of fuzziness. A probabilistic approach however can allow the development team to determine likely completion time.

Additional guidance for handling uncertainty within release planning can be found in (Cohn, 2006). The author discusses the use of both a feature buffer and a schedule buffer. When using a feature buffer the team first commit to a set of user stories to be completed within the next release. The remaining stories are placed in a buffer, if time allows these will be completed. A schedule buffer is different in that it acknowledges the uncertainty within the estimates provided by the team. Using a schedule buffer developers are asked to provide both a 50% estimate and a 90% estimate for the size of each feature. Using these two values developers are able to determine the additional time to allow for the project to ensure completion with 90% certainty.

3 OVERVIEW

Due to the nature of software development projects uncertainty is an inherent problem (Ziv et al., 1996). The method proposed herein provides key stakeholders with the opportunity to manage in a more effective manner the uncertainty in the release planning process. It has been designed with two scenarios in mind. The first scenario exists when the development team have a preconceived plan. In this situation the methodology can be used to determine likely value and the time required to complete the project to a satisfactory probability.

The second scenario attempts to automate the process of story assignment and evaluation. In the event that an optimal plan is not clear to the development team, the methodology can propose a set of story combinations. It is not designed to generate a single optimal combination of stories; rather it is concerned with developing a set of story combinations which are optimal or near optimal. The decision makers can then choose from these combinations. In this way the method guides the decision makers, an approach advocated in many works (Ruhe & Saliu, 2005).

Our method is compatible with the existing planning game in XP and starts with the current practices of gathering all user stories and estimating both the size of each story, expected value and also project velocity. The method recognises that these values are subject to uncertainty. The business value of stories can be particularly problematic for development teams to estimate, due to the high variation in possible monetary return. Similarly, project velocity can change from iteration to iteration resulting in differing amounts of work being carried out in each iteration. This can be caused by members of the core development team having to temporarily leave the project to focus on other activities such as supporting existing software systems. This is particularly true of small firms.

The methodology allows for uncertainty in three key measures by first eliciting from the development and management team optimistic, pessimistic and most likely values for story sizes, business value and the project velocity.

Once distributions are known, Monte Carlo simulation is performed to obtain the distribution for the real time to complete a selection of stories in a release. Similarly, the distribution for the combined business value of the stories can be obtained. In this way the stakeholders can explore the merits of various release plans in terms of the likelihood of returns and the likelihood of completion on time.

Currently the model can use a Triangular or a PERT distribution to represent the possible uncertainty within all estimates. Likely completion time and project value can be statistically simulated from either of these distributions based on minimum, most likely and maximum estimates. The Triangular probability distribution is well recognized as a suitable distribution when the true distribution of data is unknown. The PERT distribution is similar to the triangular and preferred in cases where the extreme values are asymmetrically spread about the mode.

4 METHODOLOGY

4.1 Identification

The process begins with the identification of all possible user stories. As with XP's Planning Game this process should involve the entire development team and a customer representative called the product owner. In an ideal situation the product owner will be an end user of the product or actual project customer. However, more often than not the product owner is a member of the sales or management team who have expert knowledge of the market and customer needs.

Once all the candidate user stories have been identified the size of each story is estimated by the development team. Unlike traditional agile methods this research suggests a finer level of granularity be used and that at this point the constituent tasks of each story be identified. The advantage of this approach is twofold. Firstly overlap between stories can be easily recognized and isolated, simplifying the dependencies that may exist between stories. Secondly this approach encourages developers to examine the underlying architecture of the project (Nord et al., 2000) and places them in a better position to provide more accurate estimates. Once all tasks have been identified the development team is asked to estimate the size of each task in ideal development days. Traditionally developers are asked to estimate single values, however, to allow for uncertainty in the size of stories, this methodology asks for the provision of three estimates, a most likely, a pessimistic and an optimistic value, in ideal days for the size of each task.

Next the development team estimates how much work can be carried out within a single iteration. This is known as the project velocity and can be found by examining previous iterations while taking into account the experience of the development team. Similar planning approaches are used in other agile methods with extensive guidance given in (Cohn, 2006) and (Beck & Andres, 2001). Due to uncertain nature of these estimates and the variation across iterations, the team is again asked to provide most likely, pessimistic and optimistic values.

With both story size estimates and the expected velocity in hand the team estimates the business value of each story. Due to the complexity of providing monetary estimates for software projects, a simplified 1 to 10 scale is used (Cohn, 2006). This technique allows the team to express the value of a story in relation to others (Boehm, 1981). For example in the event that a story was assigned a value of 2 it is half the value of a story assigned 4. Once again to allow for the inherent uncertainty within these values a most likely, pessimistic and optimistic values are elicited for each user story is required. Another factor which can adversely affect the value of a story is the release in which it is completed. Delaying the time to market of a particular feature can reduce its effective return. To allow for this, the methodology asks the team to provide a weighting in the range 0 to 1 to each story in the event it is completed in a release other than the first. For example taking a story with a value of 4, a development team may weight it as 0.7 in the second release. As such if this story is completed in the first release, its value will remain 4, however if it is completed in the second release its value will have decreased to 2.8.

4.2 Assignment

Once all estimations have been gathered the team is ready to begin the assignment phase. The goal of this phase is to explore possible plans by one of two techniques, either an automated process or through manually exploring plans to decide on an optimal one using a simple tool developed in Microsoft Excel.

Even for a particularly small development the number of possible plans can be extremely large. As such it may not be possible or practical for a team to determine an optimal assignment of stories, without devoting considerable time and effort. To this end, we propose the use of a Genetic Algorithm to help automate the exploration of the search space. Genetic Algorithms have been used to go effect in other optimization problems (Greer & Ruhe 2004) and (Ngo-The & Ruhe, 2007). Genetic Algorithms work on the basis of Darwinian Evolution. Over progressive generations the solution is improved through a series of selection, mutation and cross over operators.

In the event that an optimal solution is clear to the team the methodology can be used to determine the likely duration of a release and ensure the project will finish on time and to budget. To help in this evaluation process a simple tool was developed using Microsoft Excel, see Figure 1.

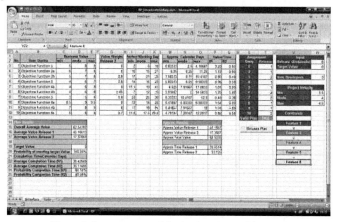

Figure 1: Screen capture of the developed spreadsheet tool

The spreadsheet is split between two worksheets, *Interface*, which contains a list of user stories, the estimated values, their weighting and input fields and *Tasks* which contain both task breakup for each user story and the estimated time for each task. Using the input fields on the *Interface* worksheet the team can assign a story to a release, set the size of each release and also set a target business value. Once a story has been assigned, the sheet, based on the most likely size and business values inputted, returns the average time and value for stories in each of the releases as well as the most likely total value and time to complete all the selected stories. These values should only be used as a rough guide as they do not represent the full distributions for the provided data.

Additionally the sheet determines the validity of the proposed plan by checking the assignment of stories to releases against any constraints which have been provided. In the event that an assignment is invalid the user is notified.

When the team is satisfied with the story assignment they can then use simulation to obtain distributions for the time and value of selected stories. Once the simulation has been completed the worksheet shows the probability of completing the given plan within the target release size and also the probability of achieving the target business value. In the event that the assignment is judged to be of insufficient quality the team can adjust the story assignment and simulate the plan again. Once a plan of sufficient quality is found and the development team is confident in its quality the plan can then be put into practice.

25

4.3 Iteration

Currently the methodology does not dictate the order in which tasks are to be completed, instead it is more concerned with determining which stories to complete in each release to maximise business value and minimize risk. Iteration planning as opposed to Release planning requires considerable more understanding of the technical requirements of a story, and also the skills of each individual within the team. While the methodology could be adopted to account for the extra data required, it is questionable whether the significant additional planning time associated with such an approach would be consistent with agile techniques.

During the course of development it may become apparent that, either estimations provided earlier were incorrect, or additional stories are required. Agile development methods are more adaptable than plan-driven ones and so are better at dealing with these changes. The iterative nature encourages making use of any additional information that may arise. Using this additional information the development team can update the data and re-simulate to establish the merits of the plan. Again, using the spreadsheet tool, a manual or an automated approach can be used to establish the best plan.

5 HANDLING UNCERTAINTY

Traditionally, agile methods require the development team to produce single value estimates for both story size and business value. These estimates would then be used to carry out a cost-benefit analysis in an attempt to maximise business value and minimise the risk of overrun. However, to allow for the inherent uncertainty of software projects the methodology presented here requires three estimates, a most likely, a pessimistic and an optimistic value. This technique has also been shown to more accurately follow the natural way in which people estimate values (Miller, 1997).

The technique used in this methodology takes a pure probabilistic approach. At present the model can use a Triangular or a PERT distribution to accommodate for uncertainty. Both likely completion time and business value can be statistically simulated from either of these distributions using numerical methods such as rejection sampling.

5.1 Triangular Distribution

The Triangular Distribution is a continuous distribution over a closed interval of real values. It takes three parameters, to represent the minimum, mode and maximum of the distribution.

The triangular distribution is well established as a suitable and easy to understand distribution when the true distribution of data is unknown. It is especially useful when the lower and upper boundaries are well defined. Most importantly, it is widely used in project management tools (Brighton, 2008).

5.2 PERT Distribution

An alternative to the Triangular distribution is the PERT distribution. Like the Triangular, the PERT distribution requires a minimum, most likely and maximum values. However, unlike the Triangular, the PERT distribution places a lower emphasis on the extreme values and a higher emphasis on the most likely or mode value.

5.3 Comparing Distributions

While the Triangular and PERT distribution are similar, PERT is often favoured when the distribution is heavily skewed. In software projects there are considerably more events that can delay a project as opposed to shorten the development time required. The Triangular distribution draws straight lines from the mode down to the minimum and maximum values. This places too much probability on values near the furthest extreme. On the other hand the PERT distribution draws a curve with diminishing probability as it approaches the extreme values. Figure 2 shows a comparison of the two distributions, where a is the minimum, m the most likely and b the maximum value for both distributions.

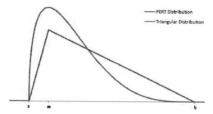

Figure 2: Comparison of Triangular and PERT Distributions

The PERT distribution places less importance on getting the maximum or minimum value precisely right. Practitioners state that this accurately models the estimating process, as estimators are more capable of providing a guess as to the most likely value with a higher degree of confidence, as opposed the extreme values.

6 CASE STUDY

To investigate the methodology two case studies have been conducted with a local company. The first of these case studies was presented in (McDaid et al., 2006) and (Logue et al., 2007) with elements of the second presented here.

The company, which to maintain confidentiality shall be titled Company Z, is a small software firm that develops a single very high value product for a small number of very large organizations. They operate on the basis of quarterly releases of their main product. Typically, a release would include new functionality driven by the needs of key customers, new functionality designed to attract new customers and modifications to improve existing functionality. They wish to be able to plan two releases in the future, selecting from a wide range of possible features for their innovative product.

Company Z uses an agile development process. While this provides them with a good understanding of the functionality that could be added to the project, they have in the past struggled to provide accurate estimates of the size of stories. This has led to time and cost overruns. These overruns have been exacerbated by the need to perform ongoing maintenance and repair work driven by the needs of their key customers, a practice that impacts on the project velocity through the amount of time that can be spent during iterations on new development.

While release planning is viewed as an important part of the development within Company Z, the plans are often flexible. These plans are driven by a set of requirements, referred to as the "wish-list", proposed by the sales team, development team and also any bugs or issues within the current release. A preference is placed on any requirements proposed by the sales team due to their close and regular communication with the customers. Currently the team find it difficult to maintain an up-to-date release plan, and scope creep is a major issue. They also find it difficult to assign business value to a particular requirement and instead rely heavily on the understanding of their sales team. When attempting to estimate the size of a release they estimate in ideal development days and make use of a schedule buffer to acknowledge risk and uncertainty. At present the size of the market and specialized nature of the developed software has allowed for a relaxed release cycle. However the organisation acknowledges a growing need for tighter and more accurate deadlines.

The second case study involved the Chief Technology Officer for the firm who, besides being an expert on the development of the candidate stories, was also, through his regular contact with customers and management, very aware of the relative business importance of the functionality. As such he provided a good representation of the product owner.

Initially, the product owner identified a number of stories for inclusion in upcoming releases. Traditionally, agile methods require the development team to produce single value estimates of the story size in story units or in ideal days. These would be developed by first splitting the story in a small number of sub-stories or tasks and aggregating the estimates for each of these. The product owner was asked to list these tasks making sure the level of granularity was chosen to isolate activities that overlap between stories. Details of the stories and tasks are given in Table 1. Information on prerequisite or co-requisite stories was also elicited. This is not presented as it is not directly relevant to the results of the case study.

Story	Tasks	Business Value		
		min	mode	max
1	1	6	8	9
2	2, 3, 4, 5, 6	6	7	8
3	7, 8, 9, 10, 11, 12, 13	5	7	8
4	14, 15, 16	4	6	7
5	17, 18, 19	4	8	9
6	20, 21, 22, 23	4	6	6
7	24	3	5	8
8	25, 26, 27, 28, 29, 30, 31, 32, 33	8.5	9	9.5
9	34, 35, 36, 37, 38, 39, 40	5	6	8
10	41, 42, 43, 44, 45	5	6	8

Table 1: Story value estimates

However, to allow for uncertainty in the size of stories, the product owner was then asked to provide three estimates, a most likely, a pessimistic and an optimistic value, in ideal days for the size of task. This data is shown in Table 2.

Next the product owner was asked to consider the likely project velocity. Existing agile practices calculate the duration of a release by dividing the size of the release by the expected project velocity. As previously discussed in this paper project velocity is often uncertain.

In the case of the organization examined it was found that the project velocity was, based on a team of three developers, estimated at 4 ideal days per 5 day working week. Arising from discussion it was found that this value could fluctuate anywhere from 3.5 ideal days up to 4.5. Therefore a minimum of 3.5 and a maximum of 4.5 were agreed.

Finally, the difficult issue of the business value of the candidate stories was addressed. Again, minimum, most likely and maximum values were elicited, this time on a scale of 1 to 10 which should reflect the likely long term financial return of developing the features. Provision of these values, which must combine short term initial return with longer term resulting business, proved a difficult task for the participant. The values elicited are shown in Table 1.

Having obtained the required data, the study then addressed whether the methodology, which provides the stakeholder with information on the uncertainty of planning outcomes, can support the decision maker under two different release planning scenarios. In the first scenario, the study looked at the length of release that should be planned for a specified combination of stories. In the second part, which shall be described later, it asked what functionality should be selected for inclusion in a release of a fixed duration. The case of more than one release was also examined but this work is not detailed here.

Task	Min	Mode	Max	Task	Min	Mode	Max	Task	Min	Mode	Max
1	2	6	10	16	3	4	8	31	2	3	4
2	3	3	4	17	8	10	25	32	0.5	0.5	1
3	4	4	10	18	0.1	4	10	33	0.5	0.5	1
4	4	4	4	19	3	5	6	34	4	8	10
5	3	3	8	20	2	3	15	35	1	1	1
6	1	1	1	21	2	2	2	36	2	3	4
7	4	4	5	22	1	2	3	37	1	1	1
8	2	2	2	23	2	5	15	38	3	4	5
9	2	2	2	24	20	25	30	39	1	1	1
10	5	6	7	25	1	1	3	40	1	1	2
11	2	2	2	26	3	3	4	41	0.5	0.5	0.5
12	1	1	1	27	3	3	5	42	6	10	15
13	1	4	6	28	1	1	2	43	3	5	10
14	3	3	4	29	1	1	2	44	1	1	3
15	8	8	11	30	1	1	1	45	1	1	1

Table 2: Task Details

The product owner decided that the first release should include Stories 1, 2, 4, 5, 8 and 9. This would involve the completion of the tasks 1-6, 14-19 and 25-40. The methodology took these stories and their constituent tasks and yielded a distribution indicating how long it would take to develop these stories. To determine the distribution for the development time of a release, each individual task time is simulated and the resulting values added. This gives one possible size in ideal days for the release. Repeating this process over a large number of runs, 10,000 say, results in a distribution for the size of the release. The distribution for the selected stories is shown in Figure 3. This shows that the size of the selected combination of stories can range from 80 to 110 ideal days.

To establish the real time it might take to develop these stories the method combines, again through simulation, the uncertainty in the project velocity with the uncertainty in the size of the stories. To simulate the uncertainty in project velocity we again use the PERT distribution. In the current model these project velocity values are assumed to be independent in that a high or low velocity does not mean the next iteration will witness the same fluctuations. However, the sequential nature of agile development (Cohn, 2006) makes it possible to recalculate project velocity in the event that project velocity values are found to be inaccurate.

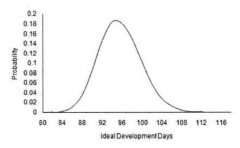

Figure 3: Ideal development days to complete plan

In this way the method can produce a distribution for the likely duration for developing the proposed plan for the next release. The distribution for the real development time for these stories is shown in Figure 4. Based on 3 developers the average time is found to be 39.4 days or 7.8 weeks. The graph shows that the real time could vary from 34 to 46 days.

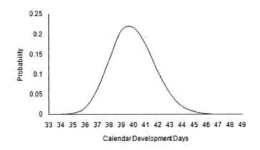

Figure 4: Calendar days to complete plan

In the case study the method was presented to the product owner through a spreadsheet tool that allowed the participant to investigate various combinations of stories to determine a best selection under different circumstances. For each combination the participant was provided with the probability of completing the tasks within different release times. In this case the data in table 3 was provided.

Iterations	6	7	8	9	10
Probability	0%	0.2%	64%	99%	100%

Table 3: Likelihood of completing plan

The tool informed him that these would take on average 39.4 calendar days and that the probability of being completed within 8 weeks was 64%. However, the table shows that, to be 90% certain of completing the desired functionality, management would have to plan a release date 9 weeks into the future. The additional 1.2 week period represents the slack time that should be included in the plan to ensure that the release is completed on time. In this scenario the participant felt that the method provided clear reasoning for the inclusion of an extra week. In practice, further slack can be added based upon the project manager's discretion.

The Case Study next addressed the selection of stories within a constrained release time. In practice, this is a very complicated decision problem that involves balancing the return on investment, as represented by the business value, with the cost of development. Assuming a release of 12 week duration the product owner was asked to use the tool to select the best combination of stories. Again, using simulation based on the PERT distribution, the tool provided information on the distribution of the business value that might result from a selected group of stories.

Following a number of iterations the participant settled on a combination that included stories 1, 2, 3, 4, 5, 8, 9 and 10, choosing to reject stories 6 and 7. The distribution for the business value of these stories is shown in Figure 5. The corresponding likelihood of achieving at least certain business values are given in table 4 below. Note that the expected business value is 58.2. For this combination the probability of completion within the 12 week release was found to be 97%.

Value	55	56	57	58	59	60
Probability	98%	92%	78%	55%	30%	11%

Table 4: Business Value

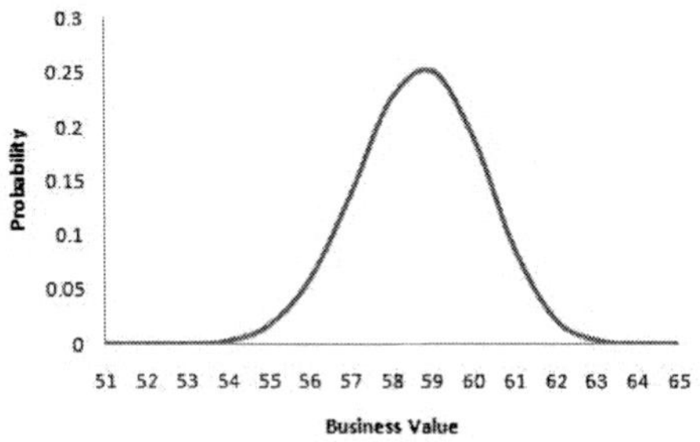

Figure 5: Business Value of plan

Following discussions it was clear that, while the product owner examined the distribution of likely business value, the participant based his decision of which plan to choose on the average business value of the combination. This was likely due to the fact that for the data provided there were not a number of plans with similar averages value. For larger release planning problems with a higher number of candidate stories, we feel the method would be of greater benefit in allowing a number of plans with similar average value to be differentiated on the basis of the return risk as represented by the distribution in business value.

7 CONCLUSION

The creation of a release plan poses a major difficulty for even the most experienced of development teams. Uncertainty in available resources and business value of candidate requirements makes prioritization a complex and daunting task. Traditional methods for handling uncertainty fail to recognise the often skewed nature of estimates. The method proposed within this paper seeks to support decision makers, it uses probabilistic methods to provide statistical distributions for the time to complete releases and the likely business value. While the method increases the data required in the planning process, it remains relatively lightweight. The method has been designed so as to fit an agile environment however it should be possible to incorporate it within most planning methodologies. The ability to update data and to easily re-evaluate a plan make it well suited for iterative and incremental development methodologies.

The development of the methodology described herein is in its early stages. While method has been shown to have some potential, there is important empirical research to be done to fine tune its application within an agile environment. Important work on the derivation of optimal plans when the number of requirements is reasonably large is also required. To this end both an ethnographic study and the derivation of a set of optimal plans will be the focus of future research by the authors

References

Beck, K., Andres, C., 2001. Extreme Programming Explained, Addison Wesley, Reading, MA.

Boehm, B., 1981. Software Engineering Economics", Prentice Hall, Eaglewood Cliffs, NJ.

Brighton Webs, 2008. Triangular Distribution [website] http://www.brighton-webs.co.uk/distributions/, February 2008

Charette, R., 2008. Why Software Fails, [website] http://spectrum.ieee.org/sep05/1685

Cohn, M., 2006. Agile Estimating and Planning, Prentice Hall.

Greer, D., Ruhe, G., 2004. Software Release Planning: An Evolutionary and Iterative Approach, J. Information and Software Technology, vol. 46, issue 4.

Johnson, J., 2006. My Life is Failure: 100 Things You Should Know to be a Successful Project Leader, Standish Group International.

Jung, Ho-Won, 1998. Optimizing Value and Cost in Requirements Analysis, IEE Software, July / August,

Karlsson, L., Thelin, T., Regnell, B., Berander, P., Wohlin, C., 2007. Pair-wise Comparisons Versus Planning Game Partitioning – Experiments on Requirements Prioritisation Techniques, Empirical Software Engineering, Volume 12, Issue 1, pp 3-33

Karlsson, J., Ryan, K., 1997. A Cost-Value Approach for Prioritizing Requirements, IEEE Software, Volume 14,, pp. 67-74

Little, T., 2005. Context Adaptive Agility: Managing Complexity and Uncertainty, IEEE Software, April, Vol. 22, No. 2

Logue, K., McDaid, K., Greer, D. 2007. Allowing for Task Uncertainties and Dependencies in Agile Release Planning, 4th Proceedings of the Software Measurement European Forum.

McDaid, K., Greer, D. , Keenan, F., Prior, P., Taylor, P., Coleman, G., 2006. Managing Uncertainty in Agile Release Planning, Proc. 18th Int. Conference on Software Engineering and Knowledge Engineering (SEKE'06), pp 138-143.

Miller, G., 1997. OO Process and Metrics for Effort Estimation, Conference on Object Orientated Programming Systems Languages and Applications, Addendum to the 1997 ACM SIGPLAN, pp 150-151.

Ngo-The, A., Ruhe, G., 2007. A Systematic Approach for Solving the Wicked Problem of Software Release Planning, Soft Computing, Volume 12, Issue 1, pp. 95-108.

Ngo-The, A., Ruhe, G., Shen, W., 2004. Release Planning under Fuzzy Effort Constraints, icci, pp. 168-175, Third IEEE International Conference on Cognitive Informatics (ICCI'04).

Nord, R., Paulish, D., Soni, D., 2000. Planning Realistic Schedules Using Software Architecture, Software Engineering, 2000. Proceedings of the 2000 International Conference, pp. 824 – 824.

Regnell, B., Brinkkemper, S., 2005. Market-Driven Requirements Engineering for Software Products, Engineering and Managing Requirements, Springer

Ruhe, G., Saliu, O., 2005. The Art and Science of Software Relapse Planning, IEEE Software, issue 6, vol. 22, no. 6, pp 47-53.

Ziv, H., Richardson, D., Klosch, R., 1996. The Uncertainty Principle in Software Engineering, Technical Report UCI-

MODELLED ANNOTATIONS FOR FIT

David Connolly, Software Technology Research Centre, Dundalk Institute of Technology, Louth, Ireland, david.connolly@dkit.ie

Frank Keenan, Software Technology Research Centre, Dundalk Institute of Technology, Louth, Ireland, frank.keenan@dkit.ie

Abstract

The Framework for Integrated Tests (FIT) is a useful tool when conducting Acceptance Test Driven Development (ATDD). The ATDD process depends on customer interaction to define tests and tool support to automate and execute these tests against system code. With existing tools, acceptance tests are usually written from customer descriptions or rewritten from existing documentation. In this work, the challenge is to address potential difficulties encountered by often non-technical customers when learning to write FIT tables. It is proposed to support the authoring of FIT acceptance tests by developers and customers from existing digital documents using a prototype digital annotations tool.

Keywords: ATDD, FIT, Agile, Annotations.

1 INTRODUCTION

Acceptance testing is described by Sommerville (2007) as the process of testing functional requirements with "data supplied by the customer". Traditionally, with plan-driven development, this occurs as the final stage of the development process (Pressman, 2000). In contrast, Agile approaches require constant customer collaboration throughout development with part of this role to provide acceptance tests. Beck and Andres (2005) defined acceptance tests in eXtreme Programming (XP) as a part of the *User Stories* practice and are therefore written before coding of the story begins. In this context, functional tests are synonymous with acceptance tests (Sauvé and Neto, 2008). Further, Cohn (2005) recommends customers themselves specify acceptance tests with developers and testers providing support as required.

Test Driven Development (TDD) is a process that makes executable unit tests an important design artefact. TDD does not always imply XP, but it is in keeping with XP's practice of *Test-First Development (TFD)*. Jeffries and Melnik (2007) note TDD is widely practised and has many reported benefits. Adoption of TDD is made possible by tools such as JUnit.

ATDD adds to this established test-first philosophy with acceptance testing of an automated and executable nature. As with TDD, support from tools makes ATDD feasible. However, Andrea (2007) claims that existing tools exhibit several deficiencies and produce tests which are "hard to write and maintain". Andrea also calls for the next generation of functional testing tools to support writing (and reading) functional tests in multiple formats. In many organisations, business rules are documented in numerous formats. In such cases it could be advantageous to use this existing digital text to create tests, avoiding the need redefine rules and reducing opportunities for creating inconsistencies. However, ATDD is currently not well supported with tools that enable importing existing documents to create executable tests.

The purpose of this paper is to highlight how ATDD can be enhanced by creating tests though the annotation of digital documents. The next section summarises related work. This is followed by the research question and objectives. In section 4, a proposed solution is explained through use of an example.

2 RELATED WORK

Generally, the Framework for Integrated Tests (FIT) is the most accepted tool (Jain, 2008) for managing acceptance tests in agile development and therefore practising ATDD. With FIT a user places expected input and output into a tabular format; the developer then executes these against the system's production code using *fixtures*. Tests are run from a command line. Other open source tools exist including EasyAccept (Sauvé et. al., 2008) which has a script syntax that supports tests written in both tabular and sequential style. EasyAccept facilitates a process used in an educational context by Savué and Neto (2008).

Mugridge (2008) introduces a process based around a library of *fixtures* named FitLibrary, which improves FIT's "business-level expressiveness" to emphasise a "domain-driven design approach". FitNesse (2008) is a Wiki framework developed to support FIT. It facilitates the editing of FIT tables in a browser allowing non-programming experts to add content. While FIT tables can be written in any tool that can export HTML, such as Microsoft Excel, these generic tools do not have any features directly supporting the task domain. Existing tools that support either FIT or FitNesse include AutAT and FitClipse.

Schwarz et. al. (2005) noted that AutAT seeks to assist "business-side people" taking a visual approach to building Acceptance Tests. However, this approach results in the need to "export" FIT Tables with re-import not available. FitClipse (Deng, 2007) builds on FitNesse therefore tests are rendered using its wiki syntax. Indeed, it could be very useful to make the proposed solution accessible from within a FitClipse based workflow.

In the authoring process, Melnik and Maurer (2005) found that the use of FIT helped students to "learn how express requirements in a precise, unequivocal manner". When providing students with pre-written requirements, Ricca et. al. (2007) found significant improvement in understanding occurred when text descriptions were combined with FIT tables, although at the cost of additional time.

Other strategies for writing acceptance tests in a customer friendly format exist, including RSpec, which is "a Behaviour Driven Development framework for Ruby" (RSpec Development Team, 2008). It promotes a workflow that involves writing stories in a somewhat prescriptive natural language style and then manually translating these steps into Ruby. However while the authors consider this approach interesting for new stories, it has limitations such as requiring re-writes when using existing documentation or stories which were written in a non-prescriptive style.

3 RESEARCH QUESTION

The research question to be investigated in this work is *can Acceptance Test Driven Development (ATDD) be improved by supporting the elicitation of executable acceptance tests from existing digital text?* Related sub-questions include:

- Is current acceptance test authoring process hampered by existing practices, which often mean the customer is limited to writing descriptions?
- Can customer role in ATDD be improved and made more realistic?
- Is there a loss of fidelity when developers translate customer descriptions to FIT tables?
- Can accurate FIT Tables be created from existing documentation?

The research strategy will involve conducting multiple experiments designed using the *GQM Approach* (Basili et. al., 1994). The initial experiments will occur before the implementation of the prototype. In these experiments, the focus is on measuring the effects annotations have on the translation of acceptance tests by developers. Later experiments with the prototype, will measure the prototype in use, especially with respect to the validity of annotation semantics. Alongside these experiments, it is planned to conduct a case study in an appropriate setting.

4 PROPOSED SOLUTION

The problems presented can be resolved by allowing customers to identify acceptance tests from existing documents in a collaborative environment. This environment would link these descriptions to executable tests written or viewable from the same collaborative environment.

This necessitates development of a text editor add-on for FitNesse that would allow the manipulation of natural language descriptions of acceptance tests by customers. Developers and Customers could then identify key elements in the paragraph and annotate these using the add-on.

The use of annotations is proposed because it provides users a simple conceptual framework which allows users to add detail to text descriptions of tests and links to be made between descriptions and corresponding FIT Tables. Indeed standard word processors as far back as 2000 have supported web collaboration using annotations (Cadiz, 2000).

To examine this, a simple mock-up has been created for a fictitious shopping cart on a website. For this scenario, assume that the rules for credit card validation have already been defined with a snapshot from an existing document included in Figure 1. A customer either alone or in collaboration with developers could examine this to identify possible tests.

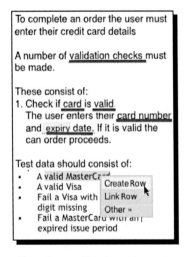

Figure 1.   Creating an Annotation

In Figure 1 for example "validation checks" could be identified as a possible suite of tests. Further, "valid" and "card" could suggest the test title. To create the test these words are annotated to form the test "ValidCard". Input test conditions for column headings can then be agreed as "card number" and "expiry date" with expected output of "Valid". The test data e.g. "valid MasterCard" is also annotated to create rows. Figure 2 shows a completed FIT Table. As the FIT table is edited, its link back to the description will be highlighted.

35

WebShop.ValidCard		
Card Number	Expiry Date	Valid?
5500000000000004	09/08	true
4111111111111111	03/08	true
4111111111111111	09/08	false
5500000000000004	03/02	false

Figure 2.   Resultant FIT Table

These tests can be printed on traditional user story cards to facilitate XP style discussion and review. Such hard copies could have the annotations represented by colour codes or simple symbols. Within the collaborative environment, bi-directional editing of generated FIT Tables and original descriptions should be permitted. Given the use of annotations, special care must be taken to handle orphaned elements. To handle translation between FIT Tables and annotated documents, both of which must first be represented by model, it is planed to evaluate using the ATLAS Transformation Language (Jouault and Kurtev, 2005).

This proposed solution will involve server-side Java to record the two-way transformations between annotated document and FIT table. Owing to the nature of the plug-in, extensive in-browser JavaScript will be required, towards this end the possibility of using a recent free open source web app framework especially one featuring an extensible rich text editor such as the Google Web Toolkit (GWT) or dojo will be considered. Given the server-side use of Java, GWT is the strongest candidate, as web apps using it are primarily written in Java with esoteric requirements written in JavaScript using a *JavaScript Native Interface*. GWT acts as a cross browser compatible Java to JavaScript compiler. However the fewer external requirements imposed by the plug-in, the more likely it is to be useful to third parties.

This combination should facilitate rapid editing of the acceptance test description and executable components allowing the team to converge on accurate tests. The environment would provide a warning when the acceptance test description requires updating fixtures with, for example, code changes. Progress to-date has included a poster that presented a solution allowing for the electronic creation of user stories from HTML documents (Connolly et. al., 2008). In this solution user stories were tagged to represent related stories.

5   CONCLUSIONS AND FUTURE WORK

This paper has argued that tools supporting ATDD need to take more account of potential customer use and that ATDD can be enhanced by allowing tests to be created from existing documents. Additionally this helps in reducing the possibility of specifying tests incorrectly and of clarifying existing business rules. The solution proposed in section 4 will seek to achieve this by allowing users to create tests through digital annotations. Guided by the research question in section 3, the focus of future work will be on the correct identification of required features and adoption of an accurate model of both FIT Tables and the annotated documents with corresponding translations. The implementation of the solution will be followed in due course by an evaluation of the process.

As a first step towards firmly establishing the design of the prototype, an experiment considering the value of annotated documents in authoring FIT Tables is in progress. It focuses on establishing the impact of the prototype's annotation in the case of a developer translating a customer-annotated description; this will help to establish the relative value of features from a developer's perspective.

References

Andrea, J. (2007). Envisioning the next generation of functional testing tools.
IEEE Software, volume 24(03), pages 58–66.

Beck, K. and C. Andres (2005). Extreme Programming Explained: Embrace Change, 2nd ed, Addison Wesley, Boston.

Cadiz, J. J., Gupta, A., and Grudin, J. (2000). Using web annotations for asynchronous collaboration around documents. In CSCW '00: Proceedings of the 2000 ACM conference on Computer Supported Cooperative Work, pp. 309–318, ACM.

Cohn, M. (2005). User Stories Applied. Addison-Wesley, Boston.

Connolly, D., Keenan, F., and Ryder, B. (2008). Tag oriented agile requirements identification. In ECBS '08: 15th IEEE International Conference on Engineering of Computer-Based Systems, pages 497–498.

Cunningham, W. (2008). FIT: Framework for Integrated Testing. Website, URL last retrieved 21st April, 2008: http://fit.c2.org.

Deng, C., Wilson, P., and Maurer, F. (2007). FitClipse: A FIT-based Eclipse plug-in for Executable Acceptance Test Driven Development. In proceedings of the 8th International Conference on Agile Processes in Software Engineering and eXtreme Programming (XP 2007).

FitNesse.org. Website, URL last retrieved 7th February 2008: http://fitnesse.org

Jain, N. (2008) Acceptance Test Driven Development. Presentation URL last retrieved 30th April 2008. http://www.slideshare.net/nashjain/acceptance-test-driven-development-350264/

Jeffries, R. and Melnik, G. (2007). Guest editors' introduction: TDD–the art of fearless programming. IEEE Software, volume 24(3), pages 24–30.

Jouault, F. and Kurtev, I. (2005). Transforming models with ATL. In Proceedings of the Model Transformations in Practice Workshop at MoDELS 2005, Montego Bay, Jamaica.

Melnik, G. and Maurer, F. (2005). The practice of specifying requirements using executable acceptance tests in computer science courses. In OOPSLA '05: Companion to the 20th annual ACM SIGPLAN conference on Object-Oriented Programming, Systems, Languages, and Applications, pages 365–370, ACM.

Pressman, R. S. (2000). Software Engineering: A Practitioner's Approach, European Adaption, 5th edition. McGraw-Hill.

Ricca, F., Torchiano, M., Ceccato, M., and Tonella, P. (2007). Talking tests: an empirical assessment of the role of FIT acceptance tests in clarifying requirements. In IWPSE '07: Ninth International Workshop on Principles of Software Evolution, pages 51–58, ACM.

Sauvé, J.P., Cirne, W., Osorinho and Coelho, R. (2008) EasyAccept Sourceforge Project. Website URL last retrieved 3rd April 2008. http://easyaccept.sourceforge.net/

Sauvé, J. P. and Neto, O. L. A. (2008). Teaching software development with ATDD and EasyAccept. In SIGCSE '08: Proceedings of the 39th SIGCSE technical symposium on Computer
Science Education, pages 542–546, ACM.

Schwarz, C., Skytteren, S. K., and Øvstetun, T. M. (2005). AutAT: an eclipse plugin for automatic acceptance testing of web applications. In OOPSLA '05: Companion to the 20th annual ACM SIGPLAN conference on Object-Oriented Programming, Systems, Languages, and Applications, pages 182–183, ACM.

Sommerville, I. (2007). Software Engineering, 8th edition, pages 80-81, Addison-Wesley.

V. R. Basili, G. Caldiera, and H. D. Rombach (1994). "The goal question metric approach," in Encyclopedia of Software Engineering, Wiley.

DEVELOPMENT OF A PROCESS REFERENCE MODEL FOR TELEMEDICINE SOFTWARE DEVELOPMENT

Jean Carlo Rossa Hauck, Universidade Federal de Santa Catarina (UFSC), Knowledge Management Engineering, Florianópolis, Santa Catarina, Brazil. jeanhauck@egc.ufsc.br

Christiane Gresse von Wangenheim, Universidade do Vale do Itajaí (UNIVALI), Computer Science, São José, Santa Catarina, Brazil. gresse@gmail.com

Aldo von Wangenheim, Universidade Federal de Santa Catarina (UFSC), Graduate Program in Computer Science, Florianópolis, Santa Catarina, Brazil. awangenh@inf.ufsc.br

Abstract

This paper presents a PhD proposal on the analysis, development and evaluation of a tailored process reference model for the assessment and improvement of software development and maintenance of asynchronous web-based diagnostic telemedicine systems based on existing standards and reference models, such as ISO/IEC 12207, ISO/IEC 15504, CMMI, ITIL, etc. Such a tailored reference model is expected to facilitate software process assessment & improvement in this specific domain as well as to contribute positively to the quality of the systems and services being developed. The current status of the PhD thesis is initially focusing on the characterization of the telemedicine domain.

Keywords: Process Reference Model, Process Assessment & Improvement, Telemedicine

1   INTRODUCTION

Telemedicine broadly refers to the use of information and telecommunication technologies to distribute information or expertise necessary for providing or delivering healthcare services among geographically separated participants, including physicians and patients [Institute of Medicine, 1996]. It allows the creation of virtual service networks, which have the potential to solve diverse problems in modern health care by increasing quality, accessibility and utilization effectiveness/efficiency as well as reducing costs [Bashshur, 1997] [U.S. Congress, 1995]. This has motivated a fast growing interest and applications of telemedicine around the world [Ronie, 2001].

Despite such potential, many telemedicine innovations are either not accepted or not successfully implemented [Bangert, 2003] [Institute of Medicine, 1996]. While various telemedicine pilot projects have been run worldwide, uptake and routine usage of such services is still subject to noticeable variations [EHTEL, 2008] [Office of Rural Health Policy, 1997]. Reasons for the problems regarding the broad diffusion of telemedicine, typically, include poor technology performance, organizational issues, financial and legal barriers [Bashshur, 2000.] [EHTEL, 2008] [Telehealth Research Project, 2008] [Paul, 1999]. It is also widely recognized that users of telemedicine services, physicians and other medical staff in most cases, are notorious for their non-responsiveness and resistance to the usage of information technologies [Anderson, 2005]. Often, there also do not exist well-defined and long-term telehealth policies and coordination of telemedicine programs, which may result in premature funding termination.

Among those barriers, technological aspects of telemedicine products/services remain a challenge to the success of telemedicine projects [Paul, 1999]. Telemedicine system and services include a broad spectrum of capabilities including acquisition, storage, presentation, and management of patient information (represented in different digital forms such as video, audio, or data), and communication of this information between care facilities with the use of communications links [ISO, 2004].

And, telemedicine systems have a high criticality regarding their desired outcomes to the improvement of human health [LeRouge, 2004]. This brings a great concern about safety, reliability, privacy, security, efficiency and effectiveness of telemedicine technology. For instance, does a radiologist at a central medical center, get radiological images with the proper resolution to effectively make a correct examination result? Are the patient's data and information protected against access of non-authorized persons? Will there be no erroneous mix ups of examination results to patients?

Many of the telemedicine systems in use today are adaptations of existing teleconferencing or desk top computer systems which were originally designed for purposes other than health care delivery. Although the system's individual components, such as software, may be regulated for safety, the entire telemedicine system is not necessarily evaluated objectively for its ability to safely provide diagnostic information. To further complicate the problem, telemedicine needs and practices are widely diverse and rapidly changing.

Given these concerns, there exists a legitimate interest in protecting the public from unsafe and untested telemedicine technologies. However, so far, there is no official telemedicine standard [ISO, 2004]. So, commonly the telemedicine industry uses high-level health care guidelines and technical standards developed for various technology sectors including multimedia conferencing, information technology, data communications, and security. In this context, basically, three types of guidelines can be identified: clinical, operational and technical [Loane, 2002]. Clinical guidelines addressing specific medical specialities, e.g., for teleradiology, telepsychiatry, surgical telemedicine or teledermatology. Operational guidelines focus on providing guidance on email communication, Internet access and videoconferencing, whereas technical guidelines cover specific aspects, such as interoperability, security, privacy, etc. Well-known examples, include DICOM (Digital Imaging and Communications in Medicine), a standard for the transfer of radiologic images and other medical information and HL7, a standard for the electronic interchange of clinical, financial and administrative information among independent health care oriented computer systems. However, the scarcity of guidelines and standards is still not comprehensive for the development of routine telemedicine products or services [Loane, 2002].

Yet, concerning the assessment and improvement of the software process for the development and maintenance of telemedicine systems and services is, basically, not covered by any standard so far. Such a standard or reference model is important when visioning the improvement of the product/ service quality as a result of a mature process executed for its development and maintenance. In this respect, there exist various well-accepted generic standards reference models focusing on software process assessment and improvement, including the CMMI framework [CMMI Product Team, 2006], ISO/IEC 12207 [ISO/IEC, 2008]/ ISO/IEC 15504 [ISO/IEC, 2005], or ITIL [ITIL, 2008]. However, as being generic models, they do not provide specific support for telemedicine products or services. A step in this direction is the MEDI SPICE initiative, which is initiating work on a customisation of ISO/IEC 15504 for the development of medical devices [McCaffery, 2007].

In this context, the research objective of this work is to develop a customized reference process model for the development and maintenance of telemedicine software and services based on existing standards and models, such as ISO/IEC 12207, ISO/IEC 15504, CMMI framework, ITIL, etc. Such a tailored reference model is expected to facilitate software process assessment

& improvement in this specific domain as well as to contribute positively to the quality of the systems and services being developed.

2 TELEMEDICINE

Telemedicine is broadly defined as the use of information technology to deliver health care services and information from one location to another, geographically separated location [U.S. General Accounting Office, 1997] [Institute of Medicine, 1996]. More particularly, these services can speed up diagnosis and therapeutic care delivery for emergencies, support virtual hospitals in patients' homes and allow primary healthcare providers in geographically dispersed locations to receive continuous assistance from specialised coordination centres.

Telemedicine covers a wide range of services and applications, and, while there is much disagreement about definitions [Tulu, 2005], telemedicine generally involves two general application purposes: clinical and non-clinical applications. Clinical applications of telemedicine can be classified as [Tulu, 2005]: Triage, Diagnostic, Non-Surgical Treatment, Surgical Treatment, Consultation, Monitoring, Provision of specialty care, Supervision of primary care. Non-clinical purposes include medical education, research, administrative meetings.

Telemedicine can be applied for diverse medical specialties, including, for example,: Home Care, Microbiology and Immunology, Cardiology, Ophthalmology, Mental Health, Pathology, Dermatology, Radiology, Emergency Room, Pediatrics, etc. [Tulu, 2005].

Another aspect is the physical environment that the physician or patient will be using during the telemedicine event. This can range from a patient at a primary care hospital to a mobile patient, or a professional at a fully equipped hospital to a professional being reached at home [Tulu, 2005].

Delivery options refer to the applications provided to conduct a telemedicine event. In general, these events are classified in [Maheu, 2001.] [Coiera, 1997]: (1) synchronous (real time) and (2) asynchronous (store-and-forward) events. Information transactions that occur among two or more number of participants simultaneously are called synchronous communications, e.g., telemedicine through telephone calls or robotic surgery. It requires the presence of both parties at the same time and a communications link between them that allows a real-time interaction to take place. Video-conferencing equipment is one of the most common forms in synchronous telemedicine. There are also peripheral devices which can be attached to computers or the video-conferencing equipment which can aid in an interactive examination, such as, e.g., a tele-stethoscope. In asynchronous communications these transactions occur at different points in time [Glueckauf, 2002]. Store-and-forward telemedicine involves acquiring medical data (like medical images, biosignals, etc) and then transmitting this data to a doctor or medical specialist at a convenient time for assessment offline. It does not require the presence of both parties at the same time.

The actual communication infrastructure can range from wired networks, radio waves, fiber optic lines, and many other forms of telecommunication technologies [Paul, 1999].

2.1 Focus on asynchronous web-based diagnostic telemedicine systems

In this broad field of telemedicine applications, we focus our research on asynchronous web-based diagnostic telemedicine systems. Such systems serve for the consultation of one (or more) distant health care professional(s) by a locally present health care professional about a patient's case, diagnosis and treatment a web-based telemedicine system to bridge the spatial distance between the two (or more) participants. Such systems offers opportunities of improving cooperation, especially among healthcare professionals, and simultaneously enhances the quality of patient care. Teleconsultations are increasingly used in those specialist fields of medicine, in which corresponding diagnostic findings data (mainly images) can be transmitted digitally, such as teleradiology, telecardiology, or teledermatology. For example, in the state of Santa Catarina/Brazil, a public asynchronous web-based telemedicine network is being build up that performs store-and-forward and examination and findings reports delivery in the fields of: clinical laboratory analysis, radiology (MR, OS, CT, SPECT, densitometry) endoscopy and colonoscopy, and EKG, besides asynchronous emergency assessment, mainly on trauma cases [Maia, 2006]. Today, the network interconnects already more than 80 hospitals and primary health care facilities in 73 cities.

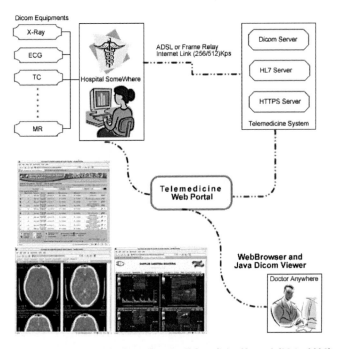

Santa Catarina State Telemedicine Network

Figure 1. Conception of the Santa Catarina Telemedicine Network [Maia, 2006]

Asynchronous telemedicine systems are gaining increased acceptance and are becoming a preferred method, e.g., for obtaining second opinions of highly specialised physicians [EHTEL, 2008], as they do not require the simultaneous presence of doctors, required, for example, in teleconsultations via videoconference, which generally is extremely difficult as the likelihood of all physicians being available at the same time is a rarity. In addition, access to emerging telemedicine applications, such as tele-diagnosis and tele-care, is an issue of great concern to remotely situated primary health care facilities. However, economic considerations and infrequent consultation sessions may make the installation of high-speed lines required to provide remote facilities with these much-needed services impossible. On the other side, asynchronous web-based systems generally require less infrastructure including lower bandwidth for the purpose of batch mode diagnosis, operating over low-data rate communication lines.

A typical workflow of such asynchronous web-based diagnostic telemedicine systems is:
1. A patient is examined at a remote health care facility (hospital, primary health care facility, clinic, etc.) by a doctor, non-medical technical personnel or nurse. The examination is captured as an electronic file.
2. The examination and accompanying medical notes on the patient's medical record are sent electronically to a central telemedicine server and become available for medical staff responsible for tele-diagnosis.
3. The responsible medical doctor/specialist analyses the examination and notes in order to indicate findings and stores the findings together with the examination information on the central telemedicine server.
4. The examination information and findings become available for the requesting physician and the regulating commission.
5. The requesting physician analyses the examination and findings and provides a diagnosis and continues the patient's treatment.

From a technology standpoint, telemedicine is the application of telecommunications and computer technologies that are already in use in other industries [U.S. General Accounting Office, 1997] [Institute of Medicine, 1996] [Perednia, 1995]. The technology includes the hardware, software, and communications link of the telemedicine project. The technology infrastructure is a telecommunications network with input and output devices at each connected location. An example of typical architecture of web-based asynchronous diagnostic telemedicine systems is shown in figure 2.

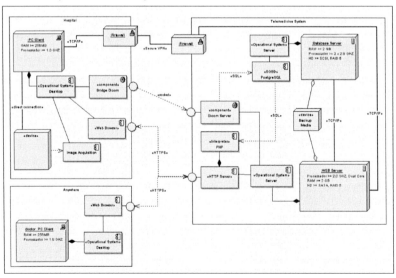

Figure 2. Architecture of web-based asynchronous diagnostic telemedicine systems

3   RESEARCH QUESTIONS

Based on the identified need for a tailored process reference model for the development and maintenance of telemedicine software systems in order to guide software process assessment and improvement, the research questions of this work are:

- Is it possible to tailor existing standards and reference models adequately to guide the assessment and improvement of the software development and maintenance process for asynchronous web-based telemedicine diagnosis systems?
- Does the existence of such a tailored reference model facilitate the improvement of software processes in such a context and improve the results of the process improvement?
- Does the existence of such a tailored reference model contribute positively to the quality of software systems/services produced by a process being improved in alignment with the reference model?

4   OBJECTIVES

The objective of this research work is to analyse, develop and evaluate a tailored reference model for the assessment and improvement of the software development and maintenance of asynchronous web-based telemedicine diagnosis systems based on existing models such as CMMI framework, ISO/IEC 12207, ISO/IEC 15504, ITIL, etc..

Specific objectives to be achieved are:

- O1. Identification and analysis of stakeholder needs and quality requirements to asynchronous web-based telemedicine diagnosis systems
- O2. Identification of relevant processes and process capabilities based on existing models and standards in order to fulfil the identified needs and quality requirements creating tailored target profiles
- O3. Development of a tailored process reference model by adapting existing models and standards
- O4. Evaluation of the defined target profiles and the tailored process reference model with respect to its adequacy and its contribution to process assessment and improvement as well as the quality of the systems/services being developed.

5   RESEARCH DESIGN AND METHODOLOGY

The present research can be classified as applied research focusing on the creation of knowledge on the application of the results in practice directed to the solution of specific problems. The research approach to be adopted is of qualitative nature rather than quantitative, which would exceed the scope of this research work.

As, so far, there does not exists any detailed method for the customization of existing standards or reference models to specific domains, we adapt an iterative research methodology to develop tailored target profiles and process reference model.

The importance of software processes and their capability is lastly determined by quality requirements to the product/services to be provided to the user/clients. Therefore, we initiate the research by developing a detailed understanding on quality requirements to asynchronous web-based diagnostic telemedicine diagnosis systems, similar to the methodology applied in [LeRouge, 2004]. In a first step, relevant quality issues will be elicitated based on a literature review and a small number of explorative stakeholder interviews. These opinions will then analysed and systematically transformed into quality requirements. In a second step, we will validate and prioritize these identified quality requirements through a broader stakeholder survey via questionnaires, involving various types of stakeholders, such as physicians, technical personnel, nurses, researchers, regulation responsibles, etc.

Then, in order to map the identified and priorized quality requirements to relevant processes and process capabilities, we intend to use an adaptation of the Quality Function Deployment method (QFD) [Akao, 2004]. QFD is an overall concept that provides a means of translating customer requirements into the appropriate technical requirements for each stage of product development and production. This is expected to provide a systematic approach for mapping the requirements and to identify relevant processes and their respective capabilities. The initial mapping done by the researcher will be validated through interviews with several SPI experts.

The identified mapping will then be used as a basis to derive tailored target profiles for this specific domain. In accordance to the identified relevant processes, existing models will be adapted/enhanced as necessary.

The resulting target profiles and process reference model will then be applied and evaluated through trial runs in practice, for example, in the telemedicine group CYCLOPS [CYCLOPS, 2008] at the Federal University of Santa Catarina. During the trial runs, data will be collected and analysed with regard to the research questions in order to evaluate the adequacy and improvement potential of the developed reference model and target profiles.

6 WORK PLAN AND SCHEDULE

This research work is just being initiated and currently we are still working on a detailed contextualization and characterization of the telemedicine domain.

Based on the planned research methodology, the research schedule is planned as follows:

1.1 Contextualization of telemedicine domain
1.2 Literature review on related work

2.1 Literature review/stakeholder interviews on opinions on needs and quality requirements on telemedicine software/ services
2.2 Analysis of opinions on needs and quality requirements on telemedicine software/ services
2.3 Validation and priorization of needs and quality requirements through stakeholder survey
2.4 Modeling of needs and quality requirements for telemedicine software/services

3.1 Mapping of needs and quality requirements to relevant processes and capabilities
3.2 Validation of mapping

4.1 Definition of tailored target profiles
4.2 Customization of process reference model

5.1 Planning of application and evaluation
5.2 Execution of application and evaluation
5.3 Analysis and interpretation of application and evaluation results

7 CONCLUSION

As part of the PhD research is also planned an international research visit for 1 year at another research institution with actuation in this area.

Activity	2008						2009						2010						2011					
	jan feb	mar apr	may jun	jul aug	sep oct	nov dec	jan feb	mar apr	may jun	jul aug	sep oct	nov dec	jan feb	mar apr	may jun	jul aug	sep oct	nov dec	jan feb	mar apr	may jun	jul aug	sep oct	nov dec
1.1																								
1.2																								
2.1																								
2.2																								
2.3																								
2.4																								
3.1																								
3.2																								
4.1																								
4.2																								
5.1																								
5.2																								
5.3																								
6																								

Research visit

References

Akao, Y. Quality Function Deployment. Productivity Press, 2004.

Anderson, J. G. "Clearing the way for physicians' use of clinical information systems," Communications of the ACM, vol. 40, pp. 83 - 90, 1997; L. Lapointe and S. Rivard, "A Multilevel Model of Resistance to Information Technology Implementation," MIS Quarterly, vol. 29, pp. 461- 491, 2005.

Bashshur, R.L. Telemedicine and the Health Care System in Telemedicine - Theory and Practice, R.L. Bashshur, J.H. Sanders, and G.W. Shannon (eds.), Charles C. Thomas, Springfield, IL, 1997.

Bashshur, R., L. Telemedicine Nomenclature: What Does it Mean? Telemedicine Journal, vol. 6, pp. 1-3, 2000.

Bangert, D. Doktor, R. "The role of organizational culture in the management of clinical e-health systems," presented at 36th Annual Hawaii International Conference System Sciences, Island of Hawaii, U.S.A., 2003; Institute of Medicine, Telemedicine: A Guide to Assessing Telecommunications in Health Care. Washington D.C.: National Academy Press, 1996.

CYCLOPS, The Cyclops Group. http:// www.cyclops.ufsc.br, , access on March, 2008.

CMMI Product Team. CMMI for Development (CMMI-DEV), Version 1.2. Technical Report CMU/SEI-2006-TR-008, Carnegie Mellon University/ Software Engineering Institute, Pittsburgh, August 2006.

Coiera, E. Guide to Medical Informatics, The Internet and Telemedicine, First ed. London,UK: Chapman & Hall, 1997.

EHTEL - European Health Telematics Association. Sustainable Telemedicine: Paradigms for future-proof healthcare - A Briefing Paper. Version 1.0, 20 February 2008.

Glueckauf, R. L., Whitton, J. D. and Nickelson, D. W. Telehealth: The New Frontier in Rehabilitation and Health Care, in Assistive Technology: Matching Device and Consumer for Successful Rehabilitation, M. J. Scherer, Ed., 1st ed. Washington D.C.: Amarican Psychological Association, 2002.

Institute of Medicine, Telemedicine: A Guide to Assessing Telecommunications in Health Care, National Academy Press, Washington, DC, 1996.

ISO/IEC 12207: 2008, Information technology - Software life cycle processes. Int'l Organization for Standardization, 2008.

ISOIEC 15504: 2005, Information technology - Software process assessment. Int'l Organization for Standardization, 2005.

ISO/IEC 9126-1:2001, Software Engineering—Product Quality—Part 1: Quality Model, Int'l Organization for Standardization, 2001

ISO/IEC 25030:2007, Software Engineering—Software Product Quality Requirements and Evaluation (SQuaRE)—Quality Requirements, Int'l Organization for Standardization, 2007.

ISO/TR 16056-1:2004 Health informatics – Interoperability of telehealth systems and networks, 2004.

ITIL v3, 2007. http:// www.itil-officialsite.com. Access on febuary, 2008.

LeRouge, Cynthia, et al. Telemedicine Encounter Quality: Comparing Patient and Provider Perspectives of a Socio-Technical System. Proceedings of the 37th Hawaii International Conference on System Sciences, 2004

Loane, M., Wootton, R. A review of guidelines and standards for telemedicine. Journal of Telemedicine and Telecare, vol. 8, no. 2, 2002.

Maia, R. S., Wangenheim, A. von, Nobre, L. F. A Statewide Telemedicine Network for Public Health in Brazil. In Proc. of 19th IEEE Symposium on Computer Based Medical Systems - CBMS2006, Salt Lake City, 2006.

Maheu, M. M., Whitten, P. and A. Allen, E-Health, Telehealth, and Telemedicine: A Guide to Start-Up and Success, First ed. San Francisco: Jossey-Bass Inc., 2001.

McCaffery, F., Richardson, I.. MedeSPI :A Software Process Improvement Model for the medical device industry based upon ISO/IEC 15504, International SPICE Days 2007, Germany, 2007.

Office of Rural Health Policy - U.S. Department of Health and Human Services, Exploratory Evaluation of Rural Applications of Telemedicine. Rockville, MD: ORHP, 1997.

Paul, D. L. Assessing Technological Barriers to Telemedicine: Technology-Management Implications. IEEE TRANSACTIONS ON ENGINEERING MANAGEMENT, VOL. 46, NO. 3, AUGUST 1999.

Perednia D. A., Allen, A. Telemedicine technology and clinical applications. J. Amer. Med. Assoc., vol. 273, no. 6, pp. 483–488, 1995

Roine, R., Ohinmaa, A., Hailey, D. Assessing telemedicine: a systematic review of the literature, CMAJ, SEPT. 18, 2001; 165

The National First Nations Telehealth Research Project Final Report, http://www.hcsc.gc.ca/fnihb/phcph/telehealth/publications/final_report.htm, access on February, 2008.

Tulu, B. Chatterjee, S. Laxminarayan, S. A Taxonomy of Telemedicine Efforts with respect to Applications, Infrastructure, Delivery Tools, Type of Setting and Purpose. Proceedings of the 38th Hawaii International Conference on System Sciences, Island of Hawaii, 2005.

U.S. Congress, Office of Technology Assessment, "Bringing Health Care Online: The Role of Information Technologies," Office of Technology Assessment. U.S. Congress, Ed.: U.S. Government Printing Office, 1995.

U.S. General Accounting Office, Telemedicine: Federal Strategy is Needed to Guide Investments. Washington, DC: U.S. Senate, 1997.

SOFTWARE PROCESS MAINTAINCE AND EVOLUTION AN IRISH SOFTWARE VSES CASE STUDY

Shuib Bin Basri, School of Computing, Dublin City University, Dublin 9, Ireland, sbasri@computing.dcu.ie

Rory O'Connor, School of Computing, Dublin City University, Dublin 9, Ireland, roconnor@computing.dcu.ie

Abstract

This paper aims to explain the overall concept and process of the researchers PhD topic which focuses on the issues of maintenance and evolution of Software Process in Irish Software Development companies, with a special focus on Very Small Enterprises (VSEs). It discusses how an organised knowledge process and effective team organisation could influence software organizations in maintaining and evolving their software process. The research is proposing a mix method study which applies qualitative (interview and focus group techniques) and quantitative (survey questionnaire) approaches. This paper will present the main model of the present study that will drive the research.

Keywords: Software Process, Knowledge, Team Development, VSEs.

1 INTRODUCTION

In the software business, the pressure to produce a software product that is relevant with the market needs and to stay competitive is a great challenge. The productivity of the organization is heavily founded on the effectiveness of their software development process. Many researchers report there is a very significant relationship between the quality software process and producing of a quality product (Zahran, 1998; Ahern et al., 2004). Therefore a lot of software companies have attempted to improve their software process to gain these benefit. However in current dynamic business environment, improving the current software process only is not enough to ensure that the company stays competitive in the software industry. These are due to a lot of challenges and obstacles which need to be handled from many related aspects. At present software process needs to be maintained and evolved in order to ensure it is always relevant with the current needs. In this paper, the researchers will study the importance of maintaining and evolving software processes from the perspective of Irish software Very Small Enterprises (VSEs), concentrating on software knowledge management issues and effective software development team issues. This is based on the nature of software process activities which typically characterized as the knowledge intensive product (Hansen and Kautz, 2004) and a teamwork effort (Amengual and Mas, 2007).

The objective of this paper is to present the overall work of researchers PhD topic which focuses on maintenance and evolution of software process in Irish Software VSEs. In this paper, researchers aims to provide some useful information in what are the challenges that Irish software VSEs need to aware in software business nowadays. Furthermore it aims to explain the whole research process that will be followed during this research project.

In section 2, the unit of the analysis which more focussing on VSEs will be described. Section 3 describes the present finding from the previous studies. The main variables of the present research will be introduced and their relationships are describes. Section 4, introduces the model, main research question and related research hypothesis of the study. Section 5 explains the methodology and the case organization. Section 6 describes a general observation and future work of the present study.

2 RESEARCH UNIT OF ANALYSIS

The unit of analysis for this research will be the Irish Software VSEs, which employed less than 25 people (Laporte et al, 2006). According to Acs et al., (2007) software industries sector in Ireland can be divided into two categories namely the Multi-National Corporation (MNC) and the indigenous sectors. Although these type of companies are different in term of revenue and total export, but number of people been employed have distributed evenly between MNC and indigenous companies (Enterprise Ireland Report, 2005). Hence the majority of indigenous firm in Irish software industry are fall under SMEs (Green et al., 2001) and employed between 10 to 99 employees with an average about 16 employees (Crone, 2002).

3 LITERATURE REVIEW

3.1 Software Process Improvement

Software Process Improvement (SPI) has gained increasing importance in software engineering. According to Coleman (2006) the main aims of SPI are to understand the software process used in the organization and to guide the implementation of changes of that process in order to achieve specific goals such as to improve software development time, on budget and with the desired functionality. Several authors agreed that SPI has a close link between the quality of the development process and the quality of the product developed using the process (Zahran, 1998). In term of small companies, Ahern et al., (2004), found that small companies are more successful in producing a quality product if SPI fundamentals are observed closely. Meanwhile economic, people, organization and implementation are four main influencing factors in SPI (Hall et al., 2002). These factors have been agreed and discussed by several researchers (Niazi et al., 2006; Mathiassen et al., 2005). Beside that the variety of implementation factors can cause the failure of a well planned SPI initiative. Therefore action plans are needed after the assessment, and SPI should be treated as a project (Weigers, 1998). Nevertheless, it is also important to ensure that the new processes are institutionalized (Stelzer and Mellis, 1998) and not affected with a process erosion problem (Coleman, 2006). Process erosion is a situation where current software process is turning back to the old level or the current software processes are become static (Humphrey, 1989). Creating an SPI implementation methodology (Niazi et al., 2006) and setting realistic objectives which can be achieved in the foreseeable future (Stelzer and Mellis, 1998), will promote and provide coordination on these critical issues (Hall et al. 2002).

3.2 SPI Standards

In SPI, several standards have been developed by various organizations and have been discussed a lot in the SPI literature. Among the popular models in literature for SPI is the Capability Maturity Model Integration (CMMI) (CMMI Product Team, 2006) and ISO/IEC 15504 (SPICE) (ISO/IEC, 2003-2006). ISO/IEC 29110 (Laporte et al, 2006) the latest ISO standard (which still under development) is focusing specifically to the VSEs and very related with the present study. According to ISO/IEC 29110 (Laporte et al, 2006) documents, the main objective of this new standard is to assist and encourage VSEs which have less than 25 employees in assessing and improving their software process. Lack of resources in VSEs and the existing ISO standards do not address the specific needs of VSEs, are the main reasons why this new standard is being developed. Furthermore, the aims of this standard are to guide VSEs assessing their current process, to relate ISO standards to their business needs and to justify the application of the standards to their business practices (Laporte et al, 2006). Therefore, with the aims and objectives of ISO/IEC 29110, it is the proposition of this research to test potential the acceptance of this new standard among the Irish software VSEs.

3.3 SPI Lifecycle

Software process and software product development are related to each others (Cook and Wolf, 1998). In order to improve current organization software process, both activities must follow a lifecycle process. Stelzer and Mellis (1998), stated that most SPI lifecycle produced by CMMI and ISO 9000, are building based from the Shewart four steps improvement cycle for planning, executing and managing improvement program. They added that the important phase in SPI lifecycle is the changes software process phase which consists of two phases (Stelzer and Mellis, 1998), an analysing the process phase and changing the process phase. This SPI life cycle is depicted in figure 1.

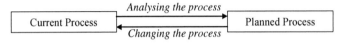

Figure 1: SPI Change Process

3.4 Process Maintenance and Evolution

In current dynamic business situation where changes happened in all sectors, software organizations need to improve, maintain and evolve their process in a way that allowed the processes to react and response to these changes environment (Borjesson and Mathiassen, 2005). It is important that organizations have a strong focus on improvement initiatives and always aware of business environment changes. These activities could support software production activities, prevent process erosion problems and will ensure that process improvement will continue (Aaen et al., 2006).

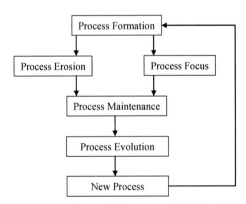

Figure 2: Software Process Maintenance and Evolution Life cycle

One factor that could continually support maintenance and evolution at a local level in software process improvement is stabilizing changed process (Stelzer and Mellis, 1998). They stressed that this effort is required because the SPI initiatives do not have along lasting effects and the benefit are often short-lived. Therefore the continuous feedback, motivation, recognition, reinforcement (Wohlwend and Rosenbaum, 1994), management commitment, opinion leader and change agent have an influence in providing continuous feedback (Trienekens et al., 2007) and preventing process erosion. Furthermore, the process of maintaining and evolving a software process also is not a straight forward task. According to Coleman (2006), a lot of factors are related and influenced in maintaining and evolving software process. He claimed that the maintenance and evolution process is an iterative process which starts with the formation of the process based on current process problem either the process is having an erosion problem or the process need more attention. Therefore this process can be depicted as in figure 2.

3.5 Knowledge Management (KM)

KM is a discipline that crosses many areas such as economics, informatics, psychology and technology. KM is seen as a strategy that creates, acquires, transfers, consolidates, shares and enhances the use of knowledge in order to improve organizational performance and survival in a business environment (Zhang and Zao, 2006). The challenges question is how to manage the knowledge and what knowledge is needed in an organization in which situation (Kukko et al, 2008). They also explained that sometime the employees do not know about all the existence and available knowledge in the organization. As a result they could not use it and utilize it for their work. Therefore specific plans such as achievable strategies, organised process and suitable tools (Dingsoyr and Conradi, 2002) will guide the knowledge management process. Furthermore, all this plans are believed could help organization in applying the old knowledge to a new situations and it is must be promoted (Kukko et al, 2008).

3.5.1 Knowledge Characteristics

Knowledge can be divided into two classes, explicit and tacit (Polanyi, 1966). Explicit knowledge is also known as a codified knowledge (Scarbrough et al. 1999) and is easier to communicate, transmit and reuse across an organization (Desouza, 2003). Tacit knowledge is highly personal knowledge that is gained through experience and deeply rooted in action, commitment and involved in a specific context (Argesti, 2000). In software engineering, individuals are the most important actor in KM, who perform tasks for achieving goal that been set by the organizational level. Through social and collaborative work among the people in an organization, process knowledge is created, shared, amplified, enlarged and justified on organizational setting (Nonaka and Takeuchi, 1995). Weick (1995) added that knowledge is about action-outcome and the effects of the firm environment. Therefore either individual or organizational, knowledge is created through a conversion between tacit knowledge and explicit knowledge as shown in SECI (Socialization, Externalization, Combination, and Internalization) model (Nonaka and Takeuchi, 1995).

3.5.2 KM Issues

As has been discussed in the previous section, knowledge is vital for every organization because it needed to perform a work in organization and when necessary need to change them. According to Hendricks and Vriens (1999) an organization cannot survived and sustained their competitiveness without knowledge. Therefore knowledge needs to manage to ensure that the right knowledge gets into the right place and so increases the innovation power of organization and its knowledge worker. As in software process which facing the problem of process loss, knowledge in organization also will be eroding over the time and will contribute to loss of knowledge in organization. The atrophy of knowledge is often implicit and its loss is often not recognizing until too late. According to Shaw et al., (2003) knowledge atrophy is referred as the loss of knowledge resulting from people leaving an organization or changing jobs within it. These situations make the knowledge became obsolete or static and leave a knowledge gap which contributes to knowledge atrophy (Bjornson and Dingsoyr, 2005). Mentoring program (Bjornson and Dingsoyr, 2005), knowledge organization via ontology and capturing knowledge via post mortem analysis method (Anquentil et al., 2006) can effect in leveraging personal knowledge and sharing between projects. This will help organization sustaining knowledge management practices in an organization (Shaw et al., 2003).

3.5.3   SPI and KM

Software process is not standardized in all software projects (Borges and Falbo, 2003). Software process must be updated and improved frequently in order to cope with any environment changes. Such environment required knowledge management in supporting software process definition and activities (Sirvio et al, 2002). Hansen and Kautz (2004) explained that SPI could strengthen knowledge management abilities for software development organization. In term of small organization, Meehan and Richardson (2002), argues that knowledge management is core to a software process improvement model. Kettunen (2003) agreed that the relationship between SPI and organizational learning are very strong. They points out that people in an organization will create, acquire and share knowledge continuously in order to improve software development practices. Therefore, it is the proposition of this research that software process issues and knowledge management issues cannot be viewed in isolation.

3.6   Software Development Teams

In software organizations, the big demand for new systems together with the increment in their complexity makes the software development process to be considered a team activity. Hence, in these organizations a teamwork interest must be seriously taken into consideration in developing a good software product. Rosen (2005) and Sommerville (2004) describe that teams are very important because this factor are among the critical factors that determine the success of the software project. Basically teams are established to solve some problem or to accomplish some task which forms the basis of team mission Team is important to increase speed, productivity, problem solving activity and organizational learning (Barnum, 2000) and give an impact to the organization and the project in order to achieve the project goal. Although the majority of software development and projects involving a lot of professional people, the technological aspect always received a lot of attention compare to the team dynamics factor (Evan, 2004). Therefore two main factors, team characteristics and team dynamics will be discussed in this paper.

3.6.1   Team characteristics

The effective team can be divided into four main characteristics; size, structure, composition and processes (Demirors et al., 1997). Several issues in team size have been identified as a critical factor in effective software teams. Gorla and Lam (2004) argues that team size is important in ensuring team performance. In general small teams are believed to function better rather than a large team. This are due to issues like lack of communication, less attention, lack of commitment and low motivation are not obvious compared to large team. Staples and Cameron (2005) stated that small teams will create a problem in solving the task because of lack of resources but big teams will need a higher coordination cost. Meanwhile, effective team structure will lead to a smooth flow of information which is related to effective communication and decision making structure. Based on Faraj and Sambamurthy (2006) an effective team structure also will bring all the important skills to software organization. Several studies argued that the effective teams are based on the team composition as key factor that can affect project performance because collective the behavioural factors such as knowledge, experience, skills and problem solving strategy will reflect a team composition in an organization (Gorla and Lam, 2004; and Shaw, 1976). The success of a project depends not only on the technical aspects but also on how effective an individual function in a team process as a whole. Effective teams are observed to perform individual members and accomplished their goals to the satisfaction of all involved (Demirors et. al, 1997). This process will lead to team interdependency in performing a team task and is a critical factor in team process (Hackman, 1987). Furthermore the equally responsibility among the team member will leads to a good coordination in team work, clear communication (Salas et al. 2000) and facilitate the social mediation of initially unshared knowledge (Faraj and Sproul, 2000). From the literatures above showed that most of the important characteristics in team are belongs and could be applied to the small software companies. Therefore it is an indication all of these factors could assist small company in improving their software development process.

3.6.2 Team Dynamics

One important aspect in teams that rarely explore by previous researchers is on team dynamics (Amengual and Mas, 2007). According to the Oxford Dictionary (1998) dynamics has been defined as "*the motive forces, physical or moral, affecting behaviour and change in any sphere*". Therefore team dynamics could be defined as an interaction between team member subject to many forces both internal and external. Team dynamics also are the hidden strengths and weakness that operate in a team between different peoples or groups. Several researchers in software engineering area found out that in an organization that team dynamics could exist because of various aspects including the task, the organizational context and team composition (Scarnati, 2001; Ayman, 2000). The presence of team dynamics characteristic in software development project could increase team productivity, enhance social interaction and communication, build team cohesion, and create a knowledge sharing environment and effective team performance (Furumo and Pearson, 2006). Therefore it is believed that this factor could help software organization especially the small company in improving their effectiveness in developing software.

3.6.3 SPI and Team

It is the proposition of this research that software process issues and team issues cannot be viewed in isolation. Software processes are related to software development and very dependent on people in execution, making decision and judgement. According to Rosen (2005) in software development, human factors are not the only important to be consider in the process but they are also a determiner in project success. Stelzer and Mellis (1998) added that people involvement in improvement activities is important because employees must adopt process innovation in their day to day activities. A quantitative survey of 120 software organizations done by Dyba (2005) argued that employee participation is the strongest influence on SPI success. The lack of involvement will disturb the improvement process because if employee did not commit themselves to all the propose change activities, the aim of process improvement will be fail (Oestreich and Webb, 1995). Therefore the involvement and full commitment from teams in process improvement is critical.

3.6.4 Team and Knowledge Management

Human resources are the important factors for effective knowledge management (Politis et al., 2003) and dynamic interaction between the team members important in knowledge creation process (Sapsed et al, 2002). Rus and Lindvall (2002) argued that knowledge management could help in managing all relevant information and knowledge that the team members contribute especially in a new product development. It also believed that a proper knowledge management process could help a team when facing process erosion and knowledge atrophy problems. Teamwork also allowed knowledge sharing within the project which depends on the strength of the cohesiveness between team members (Newell et al, 2004). Therefore it is a proposition of this research that both elements are very significant in preventing software organization from experiencing process erosion and knowledge atrophy problems.

4 RESEARCH MODEL, QUESTION AND HYPOTHESIS

4.1 Research Model

From the above discussions, a research model for this study can be depicted as in below figure 3. The figure, illustrates how two main factors; teams and knowledge management, their characteristics and relationship with SPI. The diagram showed that it is important for the software organization to have an organize knowledge process with a clear strategy, right process and correct tools. Researchers believed that with an organised knowledge process, a software process will always be updated and improved frequently in order to cope with any environment changes. Meanwhile, an organised software team development that have a balance characteristic between the technical and behaviour will help software organization in creating an effective software development team and team dynamics. These characteristics will encourage team involvement and give a full commitment in retaining, maintaining and evolving software organization software process. From the diagram, it also showed that the software teams and software knowledge management are related each other. This relationship is vital in preventing knowledge atrophy and process erosion problems. According to Salas et al, (2000) effective and dynamics team could enhance knowledge in improvement process and, with a proper knowledge management process could help teams become more effective in performing team task and making a decision (Kettunen, 2003). Aean et al., (2002) added with an appropriate knowledge creation and sharing process could provide team members with clear SPI goals and sustain their interest. Lastly, researchers proposes that the role ISO/IEC 29110 is very significant in this research due to the main objective of these standard is to assist VSEs in assessing and improving their software process. Researchers believe with the clear guidelines and procedures that been created in this standard will encourage VSEs seriously in improving their current software process.

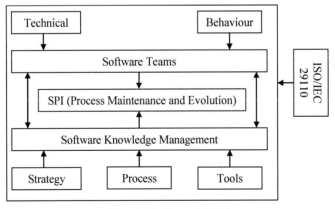

Figure 3: The Research Model

4.2 Research Question and Hypothesis

From the discussion above, the main research question and research hypothesis for this study has been established as below:

RQ: How can software development teams and software development knowledge facilitate Irish Software VSEs in maintaining and evolving software process and process improvement?

H1: There is a positive relationship between the organised management of software development knowledge, and maintaining and evolving software process in Irish software VSEs.

H2: There is a positive relationship between organized software development teams, and maintaining and evolving software process in Irish software VSEs.

H3: The organization of software development knowledge and software development teams will prevent Irish Software VSE experiencing from process atrophy and knowledge entropy problems in software process.

H4: The adoption of the proposed standard ISO/IEC 29110 will positively encourage Irish Software VSE in maintaining and evolving their software process and process improvement.

5   RESEARCH METHODOLOGY AND CASE ORGANIZATION

5.1   Research Methods

This research will applied a mix method approach (Cresswell, 1994), which is mix between the qualitative and quantitative research methods. An investigator mix method (Denzin 1989) and a sequential exploratory strategy (Cresswell 2003) will be adapted in this research. The use of quantitative will be use to explain and generalize the result of the qualitative finding. Moreover a case study method (Yin 2003) has chosen as the research strategy as to ensure the achievement of an in-depth and holistic understanding of the research phenomena (Tashakkori and Teddie, 1998). The used of multiple case studies in this research will prevent present research from the possibility of misrepresentation and also ensuring validity and reliability of data collection (Yin, 2003). Figure 4 below illustrates the above process.

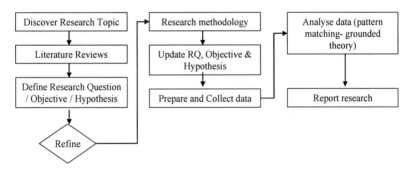

Figure 4: Overall Present Research Process

56

5.2 Data Collection Process

Five Irish software VSEs will be choose as a research samples for this study. The respondents from these companies will be divided in to 2 main categories, the management level and the software team level. The reason of the separation is to increase external validity of comparison within two groups (Kruger, 1994) and also to increase participant willingness to express their thoughts and to encourage sharing information (Kruger, 1994).

From these 5 companies, 3 Irish Software VSEs will be directly involved using the first two main methods, personal interview method and focus group method and another 2 will gather the data by using a survey method. The in depth interview will pursues a respondent subjective interpretation of a subject following a loosely structured interview guide. Respondent will also to give feedback on the related areas that not rose by the researchers. Meanwhile, the team members will be assessed by having a focus group discussion on several identified issues. The discussion will be largely free-flowing but with discreet control by the researchers. The focus group method is chosen because it is flexibility but supplicated research technique that allows soft issues been explore. According to Kruger and Casey, (2000), focus group technique is a proper way to understand and explore how people think and feel about the issues. They also added that focus groups also elicit data that allows better understanding of the difference between groups of people. The entire questions for both sessions will be prepared following the Goal, Question and Matrix (GQM) (Lethbridge et al., 2005) principle technique. This technique will start by identifying an exact goal in researchers mind, and then goal is refined into questions that usually breakdown to several major categories and these questions could help researchers in identifying one or more method in answering the questions. Therefore this method is believed could support and guide researchers in preparing and choosing suitable data collection method.

In data analysis part, grounded theory (Strauss and Corbin, 1998) coding process will be applying for this present study. The coding processes are the open coding, axial coding and selective coding. In open coding part, the researchers will analyses line by line and allocated code to the text from the interview descriptions. This will identify the relevant categories of the data. The axial coding process, the researchers will start emerge all list of code and move higher of abstract level analysis and look for relation between code. The selective coding process, this stage the researchers will more focus on the core codes which are more related to the present study. Those codes then will be combining to explain the phenomena under investigation.

6 FURTHER WORK

In this paper, the researchers has presented the overall background research effort aimed to consider process maintenance and evolution aspects as essential for software process improvement program. Firstly, the researchers have established the key process maintenance and evolution factors are essential in software process in every software organization. Then, we considered the knowledge management aspects as a critical factor in supporting software process improvement program. On the other hand, the team issues also must analysed as key important factors for both above issues due to their nature process and teams are known as a determiner factor in any software project. Since the study will focus on Irish software VSEs, ISO/IEC 29110 standard has been identified as a standard that could encourage a very small software enterprise in actively participate in software process improvement program. However to confirm these preliminary investigation, the research hypothesis must be tested and validated. To do so, qualitative and quantitative data will be collected following the research plan as discussed above. The collected data will be analyse and present in the future.

References

Aaen, I., Börjesson, A. and Mathiassen, L. (2006), "SPI Agility: How to navigate improvement projects". Software Process: Improvement and Practice, Vol.12, No. 3, pp 267-281.

Acs, Z.J, O'Gorman, C., Szerb, L. and Terjesen, S., (2007),"Could the Irish Miracle be Repeated in Hungry", Journal Small Business Economics, Vol. 28, No. 2-3, pp.123-142.

Ahern, D.M., Clouse, A and Turner, R., (2004), "CMMI Distilled: A Practical Introduction to Integrated Process Improvement", 2nd Ed. Addison Wesley.

Argesti, W., (2000), "Knowledge Management", Advances in Computers, Vol.53, pp.171-283.

Amengual, E. and Mas, A. (2007),"Software Process Improvement Through Team Management", PROFESS, pp 108-117

Anquetil, N., Oliveira, K.M, Sousa, K.D. and Dias, MGB, (2006). "Software Maintenance Seen as a Knowledge Management Issue", IST Journal,Vol. 49, Issue 5.

Ayman, R.(2000), "Impact of team diversity on collaboration dynamics, in Collaborating across Professional Boundaries", http://www.stuart.iit.edu/ipro/papers/pdf/ayman.pdf.

Barnum, C.M., (2000),"Building a Team for User Centered Design", Proceeding of IEEE, 18th Annual ACM Internal Conference on Computer Documentation :Technology &Teamwork.

Bjornson, F.O and Dingsoyr, T., (2005),"A Study of a Mentoring Program for Knowledge Transfer in a Small Software Consultancy Company" LNCS, Vol.3547, Springer

Borges L.M.S and Falbo, R.A (2003),"Managing Software Process Knowledge", Proceedings of the International Conference on CSITeA'2002, pp. 227 – 232.

Borjesson, A. and Mathiassen, L.,(2005),"Improving Software Organization: Agility challenges and Implication". Information Technology and People,Vol18,No. 4, pp 359-382.

CMMI Product Team, 2006, "CMMI for Development Version 1.2", Carnegie Mellon , Software Engineering Institute ,Pittsburg, PA.

Coleman, G., (2006),"Investigating Software Process in Practice: A Grounded Theory Perspective", PhD Thesis DCU.

Cook, J. E. and Wolf ,A. L.,(1998),"Discovering models of software processes from event-based data", ACM (TOSEM) ,Vol.7, Issue 3, pp: 215 - 249

Cresswell, J. W, (2003),"Research Design: Quantitative, Qualitative and Mix Methods Approaches (2nd Ed)", Thousand Oaks, Sage Publications.

Crone, M. (2002), "A Profile of Software Irish Industry", Northern Ireland Economic Research Center (NIERC), Belfast NI.

Demirors, E. Sarmasik, G. Demirors, O.,(1997), "The Role of Teamwork in Software Development: Microsoft Case Study", Proceedings of the 23rd EUROMICRO Conference.

Denzin, N.K, (1970)."The Research Act in Sociology: A theoretical introduction to sociological Methods". London: Butterworth.

Desouza, K.C.,(2004), "Knowledge Management : A New Commission for Industrial Engineers", Journal Industrial Management ,Vol. 46, Issue 1. p. 26.

Dingsoyr, T. and Conradi, R.,(2002)."A Survey of Case Studies of the Use of Knowledge Management in Software Engineering", International Journal of Software Engineering and Knowledge Engineering. Vol. 12, No 4, pp. 391-414.

Dyba, T., (2005)."An Empirical Investigation of the Key Factors for success in software process improvement", IEEE Transactions on Software Engineering,Vol.31,pp. 410- 424.

Enterprise Ireland, (2005), "Background to Software Irish Software Industry", http://www.nsd.ie/htm /ssii/back .htm

Evans, I (2004), "Achieving Software Quality Through Teamwork", Artech House

Faraj, S. and Sambamurthy, V., (2006). "Leadership of Information Systems Development Project", IEEE Transactions on Engineering Management, Vol. 53, No. 2.

Faraj, S. and Sproull, L., (2000),"Coordinating Expertise in Development Teams", Management Science, Vol 46 No 12 pp 1554-1568.

Furumo, K. Pearson, J.M. (2006), "An Empirical Investigation of how Trust, Cohesion and Performance Vary in Virtual and Face to Face Teams". HICSS, Vol. 1, pp. 26c- 26c

Green R, Cunningham J, Duggan I, Giblin M, Moroney M and Leo S.,(2001),"The Boundaryless Cluster: Information and Communications Technology in Ireland", Innovative Clusters: Drivers of National Innovation Systems.

Gorla, N and Lam, Y.W., (2004),"Who Should Work With Whom? Building Effective Software Project Teams", Communications of the ACM, Vol.47, Issue 6.

Hackman, J. R. (1987). "The design of work teams". Handbook of Organizational Behavior. Englewood Cliffs, NJ : Prentice-Hall, Inc., 315–42.

Hansen, B.H. and Kautz, K. (2004). "Knowledge Mapping: A Technique for Identifying Knowledge Flows in Software Organizations", LNCS. Vol. 3281

Hall, T., Rainer, A. and Baddoo, N. (2002), "Implementing Software Process improvement; An empirical Study", Software Process, Improvement and Practice, Vol. 7, No 1, pp 3-15.

Hendricks, P.HJ. and Vriens, D.J. (1999),"Knowledge-Based systems and Knowledge Management: Friends or Foe?"Journal Information and Management, Vol.35,pp.113-125.

Humphrey, W.S. (1989). "Managing Software Process", Addison Wesley, Reading, MA.

Humphrey, W.S., (1995)."A Discipline for Software Engineering",Addison Wesley, MA.

ISO/IEC, 2003-2006, ISO/IEC 15504 Information Technology, Process Assessment (Part 1-5).

Kettunen, P., (2003)."Managing embedded Software project Team Knowledge", Software, IEE Proceedings, Vol. 150, Issue.6, pp.359- 366.

Krueger, R. A.(1994)."Focus groups:A practical guide for applied research",Thousand Oaks, CA: Sage

Krueger, R. and Casey, M. (2000)."Focus Groups: A Practical Guide for Applied Research" CA: Sage.

Kukko, M., Helander, N. and Virtamen, P. (2008)," Knowledge Management in Renewing Software development Process", IEEE Proceeding, LCNS.

Laporte, C., April, A and Renault, A.(2006),"Applying ISO/IEC Software Engineering Standard in Small Setting. Historical Perspective and Initial Achievement", SPICE Conference, Luxemburg.

Lethbridge, C.T., Sim, E.S. and Singer, J. (2005)"Studying Software engineering; Data Collection, Techniques for Software Field Studies", Empirical Software Engineering, Vol.10,pp.311-34.

Mathiassen, L., Ngwenyama, O.K. and Aaen, I. (2005) "Managing change in software process improvement". Software, IEEE, Vol. 22, Issue 6, pp: 84- 91.

Meehan, B., Richardson, I.(2002),"Identification of Software Process Knowledge Management", Software Process: Improvement and Practice Vol.7, Issue 2 , pp. 47 – 55

Morgan, D.L. and Kruger, R.A. (1993), "When to use focus group and Why". In Morgan, D.L. (ed). Sucessful Focus Groups: "Advancing the state of arts". Sage, London, pp. 1-19

Newell, S., Tansley,C. and Huang, J.(2004), "Social Capital and Knowledge Integration in an ERP Project Team: The importance of Bridging and Bonding", British Journal Of Management, Vol. 15, pp. 43-57.

Niazi. M, Wilson, D. and Zowghi D. , (2006). "A framework for assisting the design of effective software process improvement implementation strategies". Journal of Systems and Software, Vol. 78, Issue 2, pp 204-222

Nonaka,I. and Takeuchi, H(1995) "The Knowledge Creating Company". Oxford University Press: NY.

Oestreich, P.C. and Webb, D.R.. (1995). "The race to level 3". Crosstalk - The Journal of Defense Software Engineering, 8, No. 6.

Polanyi. (1966), "The Tacit Dimension". London:Routledge

Politis, J.D., (2003). "The connection between trust and knowledge management: what are its implications for team performance", Journal of Knowledge Management, Vol 7, No.5, pp. 55-66.

Ramesh, B. and Tiwana, A.,(1999),"Supporting Collaborative Process Knowledge Management in New Product Development Teams", DSS, Vol. 27, Nos. 1-2, pp. 213-235.

Rosen, C.C.H. (2005) "The Influence of Intra Team relationships on the systems Development Process: A theoretical Framework of Intra-Group Dynamics.", 17th Workshop of the Psychology off Programming Interest Group, Sussex University .

Rus, I. and Lindvall, M. (2002). "Knowledge management in Software Engineering". IEEE Software, Vol. 19, Issue: 3, pp: 26-38.

Salas, E., Burke, C.S. and Cannon-Bowers, J.A.,(2000),"Teamwork: Emerging Principles", International Journal of management Reviews, Vol. 2, Issue 4, pp .339-356

Sapsed,J.,Bessant, J., Partington, D., Tranfield, D. and Young, M. (2002) ,"Teamworking and Knowledge Management: A Review of Converging Themes",Journal of Management Reviews, Vol.4, pp.71–85.

Scarborough, H., Swan, J., Preston, J., (1999)."Knowledge Management: A Literature Review: Issues in People Management".London: Institute of Personnel and Development.

Scarnati, J. T. (2001),"On becoming a team player", Team Performance Management. Vol. 7,issue 1,2 pp.: 5 – 10.

Shaw, D., Edward J.S, Baker, B and Collier PM, (2003), "Achieving Closure Through Knowledge Management", Electronic Journal on Knowledge Management ,Vol. 1, Issue 2., pp 197-204

Sirvio, S. Mantyniemi, A. Seppanen, V. (2002)." Toward a practical solution for capturing knowledge for software projects" Software, IEEE, Vol.19, Issue. 3, pp.60-62.

Staples D. S., Cameron A. F., (2005), "The Effect of Task Design, Team Characteristics, Organizational Context and Team Processes on the Performance and Attitudes of Virtual Team Members", Proceedings of the 38th Annual HICSS'05, p. 52a

Stelzer, D. and Mellis, W. (1998)."Success factors of organizational change in software process improvement". Software ,Vol.4, pp.227– 250.

Strauss, A. and Corbin, J. (1998)." Basic quantitative research: Technique and Procedure for developing grounded theory",2nd Ed, Thousand Oaks, CA:Sage

Sommerville, I.(2004), Software Engineering, 7th Edition, Addison Wesley, Reading MA.

Tashakkori, A., and Teddies, C. (1998)."Mix Methodology: Combining Quantitative and Qualitative approaches". Applied Social Research Methods, Vol. 46, Sage Publication

Trienekens, J. M., Kusters, R. J., van Genuchten, J. I. M. and Aerts, H. (2007)."Targets, drivers and metrics in software process improvement: Results of a survey in a multinational organization". Software ,Vol.15, No. 2 .

The Concise Oxford Dictionary (1998), 1st Ed. Oxford University Press.

Weick. K.E ., 1995 " Sense Making in Organization" Sage Publication Thousand Oak: CA: Sage

Wiegers, K. E. (1998) "Software Process Improvement: Eight Traps to Avoid", Crosstalk, The Journal of Defense Software Engineering.

Wigg, K.M. (1999),"Comprehensive Knowledge Management", Knowledge Research Institute

Wohlwend, H. and Rosenbaum, S. (1994), "Schlumberger's Software Improvement Program", IEEE Transaction on Software Engineering, Vol. 20, pp. 833-839.

Yin, R.K (2003), "Case Study Research. Design and Methods (3rd Ed.)", Thousand Oaks, CA: Sage

Zhang, D. and Zao, L., (2006)."Knowledge Management in Organization". Journal of Database Management, Vol.17 No.1 pp 1-8.

Zahran, S., (1998), "Software Process Improvement: Practical Guidelines for Business Success", Addison Wesley, Boston, MA.

COMBINING INTERACTION DESIGN AND AGILE METHODS FOR IMPROVED PROJECT MANAGEMENT IN INTERNET DEVELOPMENT

Namgyal Damdul, Dundalk Institute of Technology, Software Technology Research Centre (STORC), Dublin Road, Dundalk, Ireland. namgyal.damdu@dkit.ie

Frank Keenan, Dundalk Institute of Technology, Software Technology Research Centre (STORC), Dublin Road, Dundalk, Ireland. frank.keenan@dkit.ie

Abstract

Internet applications are increasingly used in everyday business and life. However, despite their obvious potential, the successful management of large-scale internet projects using traditional software project management practices has proved problematic, as demonstrated by the Irish government's eGovernment initiative. To address these weaknesses Agile Methods (AMs) for software development consider customer commitment and short development cycles as guiding principles. The intention is that close collaboration allows input from people who will actually use the final system and that the short cycles allows this feedback to influence development, thus facilitating project management. However, various difficulties have been reported with these approaches, particularly the customer role. Essentially, there are few guidelines on the implementation of the customer role to suggest how interaction with developers should occur. The research problem is to propose a systematic way of analyzing user groups and their expectations to enhance existing project management approaches within AMs, particularly for the development of internet projects.

1   INTRODUCTION

The Internet has a major influence on almost every part of our lives. Generally, Internet applications are network intensive, content-driven and continuously evolve (Pressman 2000). Internet application development is a "multidisciplinary approach requiring knowledge and expertise from different areas" (Kappel et al 2006). Here, it is difficult to have a "rigid, predefined project plan" as this would not permit a development team to "react flexibly to changing conditions" (Kappel et al 2006). Generally, internet applications are designed and developed to be used by a particular audience. Before beginning development it is best to clearly identify the main user groups and their anticipated or expected business outcomes so that subsequent effort can be more focused and better managed. However, despite widespread internet usage there are many examples of spectacular failure in the development of internet projects.

In Ireland, for example, the recent report of the Comptroller and Auditor General has highlighted the general dismal performance of the Irish government's ambitious eGovernment project (Collins 2008). Of the 161 projects approved by mid-2006, less than half (74) were fully delivered and operational. Also, almost one third (44) were only partly implemented while 23 were abandoned. Costs were 20% more than budgeted and average actual project duration was 25% more than planned. The main recommendations reported here for future internet projects were in the area of project management. Specifically, it called for appropriate use of *agile* development methodologies and the definition of *target business* benefits in advance of implementation. This however, is currently a weakness with Agile Methods (AMs).

Interaction Design (ID) is the discipline of defining the behavior of products and systems that a user can interact with (Cooper 2004). ID is concerned with making the software easy, effective and enjoyable to use (Sharp 2007). "Usability and user experience" are becoming critical factors in the success of internet applications (Constantine 2004). However, traditionally, and in contrast to agile development, ID recommends comprehensive up-front design by interaction designers before actual construction of the software by the programmers. Also, the focus with ID is on the *user* whereas with agile practitioners priority is given to the *customer*.

The research under investigation here proposes to address the following research question: *can the activities of Interaction Design (ID) be combined with Agile Methods to link the software development process to higher level goals, thereby improving the management of internet projects?*

To achieve this following objectives have been identified:
- To identify and understand the tools and activities of Interaction Design and how they are used in the industry.
- To identify and understand agile software development methods, particularly the Scrum process.
- To investigate and develop a combined ID-Scrum process to improve the requirements management.
- To test and evaluate the ID-Scrum process in an appropriate project.

2   AGILE DEVELOPMENT

Traditional *plan-driven* approaches to software development organise the main activities of *analysis*, *design*, *implementation* and *testing* in a linear manner. That is, when one activity completes for the whole project effort is then concentrated on the next with little opportunity for iteration. This clear distinction between activities, work products and roles facilitates project management. However, many problems have been reported, which has led to the recent emergence of the agile approaches – the so-called Agile Methods (AMs). Here, software is developed in short iterations throughout the project, providing an opportunity for the customer and users to evaluate a working product providing feedback, which, generally, leads to further changes to the software. Each iteration involves analysis, design, implementation and testing. AMs do not expect static requirements; rather it considers that requirements evolve during the process. Enough detail is elicited at the start of the project to allow overall project planning. Generally, AMs advocate close cooperation between interested stakeholders including business people, software developers, customer and users at the different stages of the process, and face to face communication and interaction among the development teams are preferred (Jeffries 2001). In particular, they discourage comprehensive up-front analysis and design, as the design changes are considered inevitable during the process.

2.1   Agile Project Management

Traditionally in plan-driven software development requirements are documented in "dry, formal language" that describes the software system and acts as both means of communication and data storage. However, comprehensive documentation of requirements is not always desirable because the documents are selective, unidirectional and may be ambiguous and vague (Davies 2006). In Agile software development teams "expect change, accepting that requirements will evolve throughout the project" (Ambler 2007). Extending the challenge with Web development, in particular, is more complex due to need for considering multimedia and marketing aspects in the development of requirements (Escalona and Koch 2004). Moreover, in these projects, "clients did not well understand the capabilities of the technologies" and their "own needs as they related to technology" (Lowe and Eklund 2002). It is recommended that for web development design activities and requirements elicitation should be handled and managed simultaneously.

Generally, with AMs requirements are recorded in brief format as, for example, *user stories*. A user story is a non-technical and "high-level definition of requirements, containing just enough information so that the developers can produce a reasonable estimate of the effort to implement it." (Ambler 2008). The main activities of project management are applied to these stories in consultation with the customer. Detailed project management takes place within each iteration when stories are examined in detail. Project management and requirements development evolve together.

Scrum is an overarching process for *planning* and *managing* software development projects (Martin 2004). It is a team based agile process to develop software systems iteratively and incrementally, and manage and control development work (Schwaber 2008). Work is prioritised on the basis of business value, effectiveness, increasing profit, customer needs. Integrating changing requirements is an important feature of Scrum (Sutherland and Schwaber 2007). Frequently, in practice, it is necessary to combine Scrum with other approaches that focus on programming and individual team practices, such as eXtreme Programming (XP) and FDD (Martin 2004, Kerbs 2005 and Kniberg 2007). However, Martin (Martin 2004) warns that as development in Scrum is very fast; *tight control* and *feedback* are required to keep that speed from creating quality problems. Additional practices need to be added to achieve this. In (Kerbs 2005), for example, various artifacts and activities are added to supplement Scrum.

In Scrum requirements are organized in a Product Backlog (PG), which is, essentially, a list of features requested including both functional and non-functional requirements. Anyone can add items to the list but it is prioritized only by the product owner. The items which have highest priority in PG are broken down into small chunks so that they can be estimated and testable. Frequently, user stories are used to record requirements (Schwaber 2008). For each iteration or sprint a subset of PG features are implemented. A Sprint Backlog is a list of tasks that must be completed to realize the sprint's goal. Within *Sprint Goals* are specific and measurable goals derived from the negotiation between the PO and ST.

Various roles are recommended in Scrum. The Product Owner is responsible for defining the features of the product, deciding on release date and content, prioritizing the features in accordance with market value. A Scrum Master plays the role of supporting, coaching and guiding the team through the process and is also responsible for removing obstruction faced during the process (Waters 2007). The Scrum Team, of seven or so developers, has the right to function in any manner it likes to achieve the *sprint goal* and work result specified by them (Sutherland and Schwaber 2007).

The Scrum Process is carried out in three main phases *Sprint Planning*, *Sprint Review*, and the *Daily Scrum Meeting* (Scrum Alliance 2008). A Sprint Planning Meeting (SPM) SPM begins after the Product Backlog is defined and prioritized to launch for the thirty day sprint with a detailed plan for the iteration developed. A new SPM is held after each Sprint until the whole project is completed. It is the responsibility of the Product Owner to *review the vision*, roadmap, release plan in addition to reviewing the Product Backlog with the Scrum team for estimates for features and decide how much work can be done in a sprint based on team size, time available and team's productivity. Scrum master leads the team to break down Product Backlog features into tasks which forms the individual Sprint backlog.

During development the Scrum Master leads the 15 minute long Daily Scrum Meeting (DSM) where team members assess progress by addressing three questions, *what did I do yesterday, what will I do today and what impediments got in my way?* At the Sprint conclusion a Sprint Review Meeting is held where the Product Owner demonstrates the potentially shippable code and he determines which Product Backlog items have been completed in the Sprint and discusses with the Scrum team and stakeholders to reprioritize the Product Backlog for the next Sprint.

3   INTERACTION DESIGN (ID) PROCESS

Cooper (Cooper 2004) describes the three main stages in ID as:
* Conceptual design concerns with what is valuable for the user in the first place.
* Behavioral design which concerns with how the elements of the software act and communicate.
* Interface design which concerns with the interface of the program.

Typically, interaction design tools are applied in a project to optimize the design of software. Important interaction design tools include *personas, goals* and *scenarios.* Personas are hypothetical characters which are defined with precisions after detail investigation on the potential users and are the most important design tools if applied with "some sophistication" (Cooper 2004). It is recommended that software is developed for the defined persona and not for actual user. A persona exists to achieve his *goals*, and the goals exist to give meaning to a persona and the most important goal is the personal goal which is to "not feel stupid" when interacting with the system (Cooper 2004). *Scenarios* provide descriptions of how a persona interacts with a system and scenarios are envisaged by Interact Designer who thinks in the way personas would think. Also, scenarios help in eliminating unnecessary tasks by identifying overlap and interaction.

Sharp (Sharp 2007) suggests a more evolutionary approach to ID with four main activities:

1   Identifying needs and establishing requirements for the user experience.
2   Developing alternative designs that meet those requirements.
3   Building interactive versions of the designs so that they can be communicated and assessed.
4   Evaluating what is being built throughout the process and the user experience it offers.

4   INTERACTION DESIGN AND AGILE DEVELOPMENT

Despite certain similar characteristics the two approaches differ. Significantly, interactions designers recommend that substantial design takes place up-front, at the beginning of the project, and that this changes little during development. On the other hand agile practitioners recommend minimal design at the beginning, expecting that this will evolve during development. Also, ID is *user-focused* while agile development is *customer-focused.*

Ambler (Ambler 2007) does however suggest that with minor operational changes, it is possible for Interaction Designers and Agile practitioners to work together. Broad, high-level modeling at the beginning can help to identify key issues, with the details examined in *Just-in-Time* manner during the development process.

An important issue for collaboration is that since agile development follows flexible and highly collaborative organizational strategy, the designs specified in ID are likely to be changed by software developers (Ambler 2007). ID is holistic in nature involving specialized skills while Agile is incremental involving a team of generalists.

There has been few works on combining aspects of ID with agile development. Patton (Patton 2002) described an ID-XP combined process by defining the user roles and writing their detailed tasks based on the interaction design contexts and creating an abstract prototype with the help of the user tasks. However, he does warn that this process "takes long for those who don't do it often". Blomkvist (Blomkvist 2002) explained the key aspects of the integration of HCI and agile development highlighting the need for specifying the *usability goals* that can direct the course of the iterative development and usability validation but it is reported that usability methods can be "overly elaborated" and "highly lengthy" in duration. Patton (Patton 2004) stressed the need for clarity of the goals of the users roles and a "common mistake is for tasks to "wander" in goal level – some very high level, some very low". Constantine (Constantine and Lockwood 2004) discussed about reincarnated agile usage-centered design using card based modeling and decision making and prioritizing roles and their tasks and creating prototypes and highlighted the need for a minimum up-front design. Martin (Martin 2004) used mainly Scrum for managing project and XP for development in a Scum-XP combined process. XP provided the feedback and tight control over quality in fast pace Scrum development. However, difficulties have also been reported with XP in relation to the customer role and in identifying overall goals.

5   WORK IN PROGRESS

Work to progress this research has been made on a number of fronts. A poster titled "Building a XP Metaphor" will be presented this June at XP2008 Conference in Limerick, Ireland. This examined how a group of students managed user stories to develop an internet site. Particular problems that were reported by the members were that *scope* was difficult to manage, the overall *goal* and *direction* of the project were unclear and that it was difficult to provide iteration end checks to show progress.

To overcome these difficulties a combined ID-Scrum process to enhance project management for internet development is being investigated. However, it is important that this is conducted in an agile manner particularly in terms of the time and effort required. The proposed solution uses ID to specify a high level goal and specific goals based on individual user scenarios to provide a good foundation for forming requirement lists, or stories, for the Product Backlog, as this is the crucial initial step of the Scrum process. The proposed solution shall address agile requirements development by having a shared guiding *high-level user goal* throughout the process and *specific user goals* during the individual iterations. To clarify the issues reported in the literature interviews have been arranged with experts in ID and the AMs, particularly Scrum.

The proposed ID-Scrum process for software development will be used in a case study with a group of final year computing students. During the case study, the participants will be observed and then questionnaires will be used to collect their experiences. This will be followed by interviews of the participants to learn what they think about the process.

6   CONCLUSION

The Scrum process promotes iterative software development and extensive customer interaction to facilitate project management. ID has been proposed as a candidate approach to be used in combination with Scrum to overcome the reported difficulties in agile development. In doing this it is important to remain consistent with the agile principles; any process used should not cause excess effort or delay. ID is used to support the development of the product backlog of Scrum. This helps Scrum teams to decide on the tasks for implementation based on the user goals. Sprint goals, targets for individual sprints, are derived from this and used to assist project management. Trials are being arranged to assess this approach.

References

Ambler, S. (2008), "User Stories"[Online], Available http://www w.agilemodeling.com/artifacts/userStory.htm [accessed 12th May, 2008].

Ambler, S. W. (2007), "User Experience Activities on Agile Development" [Online], http://www.agilemodeling.com/essays/agileUsability.htm [accessed 10th October, 2007].

Blomkvist, S. (2006), "User-Centred Design and Agile Development of IT Systems" [Online], Available: http://www.it.uu.se/research/publications/lic/2006-012/ [accessed 13th November, 2007].

Collins, J. (2008) "Failure of e-government" The Irish Times [Online], 11 January, available from: http://www.ireland.com/newspaper/finance/2008/0111/1199917844950.html [accessed 20 Febuary, 2008].

Constantine, L. and Lockwood L. (2004), "Usage-Centered Engineering for Web Applications", Avalaible: http://www.foruse.com/articles/webapplications.pdf [accessed 7th May, 2008].

Constantine, L. (2006), "Activity Modeling: Toward a Pragmatic Integration of Activity Theory with Usage-Centered Design", Available: http://www.foruse.com/articles/activitymodeling.pdf [accessed 30th May, 2008].

Cooper, A. (2004), "The Inmates Are Running the Asylum", Sams Publishing, Indiana.

Davies, Rachel. (2005), "Agile Requirements" [Online], Available: http://www.methodsandtools.com/archive/archive.php?id=27 [accessed 13th November, 2007].

Escalona, M.J, Koch N, (2004), "Requirements Engineering for Web Applications – A Comparative Study", http://www.pst.informatik.uni-muenchen.de/~kochn/KochEscalonaJWE-rev.pdf [accessed 20th Feb, 2008].

Jeffries, R. (2001), "What is Extreme Programming?" [Online], available from: http://www.xprogramming.com/xpmag/whatisxp.htm [accessed 30th September, 2007].

Kerbs, J. (2005), "RUP in the dialogue with Scrum" [Online], Available: http://www.128.ibm.com/developerworks/rational/library/feb05/krebs/ [accessed 27th March, 2008].

Kniberg, H. (2007), "Scrum and XP from Trenches" [Online], Available: http://www.crisp.se/henrik.kniberg/ScrumAndXpFromTheTrenches.pdf [accessed 27th March, 2008].

Lowe, D. B, Eklund, J (2002), "Client needs and the Design Process in Web Projects", http://services.eng.uts.edu.au/~dbl/archive/2003-Low03i.pdf [accessed 20th Feb, 2008].

Pressman R. S, (2000), "Software Engineering, A Practitioners Approach". Berkshire, England: McGraw-Hill Publishing Company.

Kappel. G, Proll B et al (2006), "Web Engineering", John Wiley & Sons Ltd, Germany.

Martin, R. (2004), Object Mentor Inc. "Best Practices in Scrum Project Management and XP Agile Software Development" [Online], Available: http://www.controlchaos.com/download/Primavera%20White%20Paper.pdf [accessed 14th December, 2007].

Patton, J. (2002), "Hitting the Target: Adding Interaction Design to Agile Software Development" [Online], Available: http://oopsla.acm.org/extra/pracreports/HittingTheTargeReport.pdf [accessed 13th November, 2007].

Patton, J. (2004), "Interaction Design Meets Agility: Practicing Usage-Centered Design in an Agile Software Development Environment" [Online], Available: http://www.agilealliance.com/system/article/file/1368/file.pdf [accessed 13th November, 2007].

Sharp, H. (2007), "Interaction Design: Beyond Human-Computer Interaction", John Wiley & Sons, Ltd, England.

Schwaber, K. (2008), "What is Scrum?" Available: http://www.controlchaos.com/about/ [accessed 27th March, 2008].

Scrum Alliance, (2008), "Scrum Ceremonies" Available: http://www.scrumalliance.org/view/scrum_ceremonies [accessed 2nd April, 2008]

Sutherland, J., Schwaber, K. (2007),"The Scrum Papers: Nuts, Bolts, and Origins of an Agile Process", Available: http://jeffsutherland.com/scrum/ScrumPapers.pdf [accessed 27th March, 2008].

Waters, K. (2007), "How to implement scrum in 10 easy steps" Available: http://kw-agiledevelopment.blogspot.com/2007/09/how-to-implement-scrum-in-10-easy-steps_20.html [accessed 27th March, 2008].